MASSAGE ~~NO~~ BOOM BOOM

Anand Prabhu was schooled in India and worked as a financial analyst for five years. He then did his masters from the US, spending his young adult years as a student and a writer in New York, before returning to the country of his birth. He has been a novelist, a journalist, an editor and a traveller, touring extensively across East and Southeast Asia. He is currently working on two other novels, and believes in the philosophy of tolerance and individual freedom.

MASSAGE ~~NO~~ BOOM BOOM

ANAND PRABHU

HarperCollins *Publishers* India

First published in India by
HarperCollins *Publishers* in 2012

Building 10, Tower A, 4th Floor, DLF Cyber City, Phase II,
Gurugram Haryana – 122002, India
www.harpercollins.co.in

2 4 6 8 10 9 7 5 3

ISBN: 978-93-5029-374-4

Typeset in 11.5/14.5 Perpetua by
R. Ajith Kumar

Printed and bound at
MicroPrints India, New Delhi

To all masseuses (and I include all female massage therapists) who do it for more than money, bringing compassion, love, laughter and beauty to our lives, infecting us with their generosity and goodwill.

Further, this book is dedicated to Henry Miller and all other writers who taught the author that courageously expressing the truth, as one sees it, is one of the highest duties of a writer, and an obligation owed to society.

‘What the boy had felt was something pure . . . the simple desire to reach out and touch someone, to be held lovingly in someone’s arms. Tenderness is a deeper instinct than seduction, which is why it is so difficult to give up hope.’

—Michel Houellebecq, *Elementary Particles*

‘Nature knows no indecencies. Man invents them.’

—Mark Twain, *Notebook*

‘I have [a good massage] done at least once a day or at times twice a day. I am convinced that this has kept me going for so long.’

—Khushwant Singh, writing at the age of ninety-five, *Deccan Herald*

CONTENTS

PART III: ORIENTAL MASSAGE: SOUTHEAST ASIA AND CHINA

PART IV: MASSAGE INDIAN-STYLE: THINK TWICE BEFORE SHAKING HANDS

PREFACE

'*All you need is love*'—so sang the Beatles, paraphrasing Jesus perhaps. And I believe with all my heart that a truly good and honest massage is one of the highest expressions of love, a diluted and legal edition of love without registration requirements if you will—the love, the tenderness, and the healing, soothing, affirming touch that those of us who live in the prim-and-proper sections of middle-class society often cannot easily obtain in the ordinary course of our serial monogamous, serial divorcing lives. Unable to obtain it through regular sources, we are willing to pay through our noses for strangers to touch and comfort us—and this touch and massage becomes an anodyne to the angst of modern living, the rush-hour commutes, the terror-alert upgrades, and the realization that we may have to slave for the rest of our lives to pay for the sins of Wall Street and political bandits.

For nearly twenty-five years now, I have been in love with this manifestation of love called massage, partly because I constantly suffered from acute back and body aches brought on by stress and the withdrawal effects of prescription tranquillizers, but also because of a deep hunger for touch and love. The result is this eclectic and subjective guide which makes no claim to be authoritative, scholarly, comprehensive, or to speak for anything but a highly subjective male experience (the female experience would require another writer and a different book to do it justice). It is simply an honest and uninhibited door-opener for novices, a laugh-along guide to the bewilderingly complex and exploding world of massage, which abounds in charlatans and rip-off artists, and is also moved by the desire to spread the compassion, the love and the humanity inherent in massage.

Along the way, the book is a massage travelogue taking the lay reader along on a tour through various countries, cultures and massage experiences, some very rare. And despite considerable liberalization and a sexual revolution in metropolitan India, the fundamentals haven't changed, human history being always a struggle between the forces of individual freedom and authoritarian repression and control. Regardless of whether massage is important or completely non-existent in your life, this story matters in that it illustrates the repressive forces that try to stop other people from having pleasure or freedom. This may not be your story, and yet, it is your story, if you believe in *tat tvam asi*: thou art part of the whole.

Above all, this is a book written from the heart, in the Panglossian hope that massage may one day become a basic human right, provided for in our health plan (as it already is in Canada and a few European countries), and endorsed by the United Nations.

PRELUDE: MAN'S HUNGER FOR THE BREAST

I grew up in a small and conservative south Indian town, where I had a strict Catholic upbringing so repressed that had we not been rather hard up, my mother would have made the cat, the dog and the chickens wear pants, and possibly tiny underpants beneath them, so as to shield their shameful parts from the gazes of the innocent as well as the wicked.

How could it have happened then that I not only managed to survive this childhood, but that on one 93-degree July day, twenty years later, I found myself naked and with a hard-on in a clothes-optional swimming pool at a New Hampshire spa?

My official excuse: I had come to the spa for a strictly therapeutic massage, and had been told, to my surprise, 'You're going to have to wait 45 min. Would you like to use the clothes-optional pool while you wait? It's free.'

But if you were to dig deeper into my psyche and probe my secret longings and dreams, this was exactly the kind of decadent moment I had been waiting for all my life—it was the kind of life I had come to America for in the first place.

Let me rewind the narrative a bit. In 1986, seven years after arriving in America, I was living with my wife and young child in a subsidized two-bedroom apartment in Long Island, New York—and believed I was on my way to the American Dream. My wife was a beautiful woman who kept getting more beautiful by the day, besides which she was a popular medical resident, and passionate and loving in bed and out of it. I was in my mid-thirties, with a size-32 waist, and a reasonably healthy and virile body (which I exercised at a Jack LaLanne health club), and was one-third through a novel whose initial chapters had received a head-turning reception in my Columbia University writers' workshop.

That was when I had my first full professional massage, from the Irish redhead Julia with the lovely soft skin who surrounded you with a cocoon of affection as she massaged you, the curly locks from her lush head of hair sometimes softly brushing over your skin and sending small, tingling electrical charges all through your body.

I wouldn't have dreamt it then that this would be the beginning of a long journey—a journey of flesh, touch, tenderness and eroticism consisting of over 3,500 massages received from nearly a thousand different women in over twenty countries, and sometimes culminating in wild and unexpected climaxes. Most of that exciting stuff happened later, in a different world—and not in America, the Promised Land that I had once believed was going to satisfy my secret dreams. By then, my life had changed dramatically, thanks to a series of traumatic events. All of this, the professionally excellent and loving therapeutic massages, from Julia's first one in 1986 to the later total and enveloping ones—in which, somewhere in the course of the massage, I and the masseuse would become one flesh—would provide the soft landings, the islands of love that cushioned and comforted me in the next two tumultuous decades of babies, books, drug withdrawals, depression, tragedy, divorce and part-time homelessness. Besides, of course, neck spasms, shoulder pains, sore feet, hamstrings like guitar strings, knots in the back, tense buttocks, hungry thighs, myofascial pain syndrome, and a penis that was an endless glutton for touch and comfort.

But why did my life follow this unusual path? To understand the driving force partly behind this complex and amazing tale, I need to briefly take you back to my childhood. As a weak child in India, with a body like that of Oliver Twist, frequently beaten by Catholic nuns, assorted guardians and priests, I had begun to think of the world as unfair, and of most rules as having been invented by a ruling class for its own benefit. I became a rebel for life, a rebel against rules and restrictions on freedom. Unconvinced that the nuns and priests were always fair and moral in their behaviour, I reasoned that quite possibly the opposite of what they preached was true. And I revolted against their teaching that sex was synonymous with sin.

This was the person who found himself naked and with an erection in a swimming pool populated by just one other human being—a stark naked blonde. A few months had passed after the birth of my third son, and the large riverfront house that my wife had just purchased was being commandeered by my loud mother-in-law who was on her annual green card visit. Her thunderous voice would penetrate the walls, doors and multiple floors, giving me an excuse to escape to the green and bucolic areas of New Hampshire—a land of meadows, streams, lakes and vast vistas of green, with the White Mountains visible in the distance—for a few days to write. And though I had a nearly insatiable libido in those days, this specific pocket rocket at the spa owed its existence to a large mohawk-topped pussy, displayed between wide open legs, as if its owner was inviting Ra, the sun god, to bless it. She was a thirtyish woman with one glass eye (and one real one), and full and pert size-36D breasts. She seemed to alternate between reading a mass-market paperback and smiling vaguely at no one in particular as she lay back on a beach lounger, her mildly tanned and delicately oiled skin gleaming in the sun. It was a lovely tan, such as it was, for there was no awkward white patch where the bikini might have been—the mark of a true and uninhibited sun worshipper democratically distributing wholesome sunshine to every square millimetre of her skin. I tried to avert my gaze from the fulcrum of her being and direct it instead towards her glass eye, and then up at the hazy blue sky desperately trying to spot a swallow or a flock of Canadian geese to distract myself with, not wanting to emerge from the water in my embarrassingly erect state, my rocket devoid of its camouflaging pocket. But my eyes kept getting magnetically re-attracted to the mohawk-topped treasure. For it was one of the rare times, if not the first time, that I had seen a Western woman naked, in the flesh, and I was a tongue-tied social klutz in those days, especially in America, when I was yet to discover a self-confidence that could match my erections. So it happened that my erection and that remarkable vagina were never introduced to one another, and each went home sun-kissed but otherwise lonely and unsatisfied, perhaps to be consoled by our respective hands.

Reflecting on that incident now, I credit my endless desire for massage in my American and post-American years to my insatiable yearning to be touched and loved, to be tenderly caressed and, at some secret level, to be enveloped in a sexual embrace—a yearning which initially proceeded from my pain, and later became a frantic attempt to save my life and survive the catastrophe.

This book is the story of that long journey, from being a klutz in America never managing to bed a single masseuse (except once when I was violated for a few surprised minutes by one, and one other hugely exceptional occasion), to becoming a frequent diner at many a gorgeous Southeast Asian woman's breast. It pauses occasionally for essayistic and playful explorations of the wondrous, and sometimes hilarious, nature of massage, desire and the games men and women play with each other.

But wait a minute, you ask: Breasts? You mean titties? What's going on, and how do lovely titties, God bless 'em, enter the story? This is supposed to be a book about massage, right?

All right, then. First, I will speak of massage in general, of my introduction to massage in America, and then briefly about man's hunger for the breast and its part in the story. This will be followed by an explosion of joyous and hilarious massage stories from around the world interwoven with tongue-in-cheek meditations on massage and the part it could play in bringing about world peace.

PART I

FROM MASSAGE TO SEX, FROM LOVE TO PEACE

1

MASSAGE NO BOOM BOOM

I am no saint, and long ago gave up any illusions that I would ever become one, after having failed miserably at it in my childhood years; nor am I, or ever will be, a spectacular sinner like Dubya Bush, Dick Cheney, Mick Jagger or Genghis Khan. I am what I am—and I just try to be as honest as I can be most of the time.

So, despite my knee-jerk tendency to be defensive and moralistic at times, a habit arising from having lived so long in a hypocritical society and having internalized its inquisitors and tormentors, having had them burned into my internal hard drive, I was never as straight as I thought I was, or pretended to be. Maybe it was God's plan for me that I should be a sinner so that the pure and the virtuous may have someone to feel superior to.

Still, for nearly fourteen years, beginning in the United States around 1986, I fooled myself into believing that massage and sex existed in separate, watertight compartments: I received my massage on massage tables from professionals, and I received my sex at home in bed from my beautiful and talented wife (well, a few times on the sofa or on a rug too, but never on the kitchen table). With rare exceptions, I responded scornfully and disapprovingly whenever someone tried to offer me massage and sex together in various creative 'combo' packages. (Except for one hilarious accident, it was relatively easy not to get confused. If the massage cost significantly more than forty-five to sixty dollars an hour, or if the advertisement used overly suggestive language or had illustrations of panting, semi-undressed women with a few loose buttons and parted lips, it was probably going to be something other than just a massage.) Though I was aroused more than half the time during my various massages, I didn't need to burden myself with unnecessary guilt, considering that I had, on the whole, a good marriage.

Still, excluding half-a-dozen accidental episodes, my 1,500 massages up until 1999 were all 100 per cent 'legitimate', though a handful of these masseuses, rather sensibly, didn't bother with towels. But around the turn of the millennium, things began to change when something happened in my life.

It was more than that I ceased to have an official wife; it was that my whole life started to fall apart, and from that point on, finding the company and touch of women to be deeply therapeutic to body and soul, in whatever form it was offered (and sometimes given without asking), I found myself quickly surrendering my hauteur and morally righteous disdain for sensual or ecstatic massage. When, for example, a masseuse's hands strayed under the towel to gently brush the bulb or head of my penis each time she made a downward movement over my thigh, and repeated this action twenty times, I didn't raise my hand and shout, 'Objection, Madam!' I accepted it as a gift, as an act of comfort, as a deep handshake between our souls. And sometimes, when a gift such as this developed into something more profound, and led to a mutually pleasurable merging of body and soul, erasing the illusion of separateness, for anywhere between fifteen and thirty minutes, I didn't object to that either. It still didn't happen too often, but I slowly realized that my religious and fanatic insistence on 'pure unadulterated massage' was partial bullshit. For the spirit wants what it wants, or needs (and sometimes the spirit wants just spirits, and massage is beyond the thoughts of a man whose insides are drenched with distilled spirits). Therefore, no absolutist and big-brotherly moral code of one section of society should Nazi-boot out one of the most salubrious and life-giving—and sometimes, life-saving—pleasures in other people's lives.

What a slow learner I was, for it took me twenty years of being massaged by about 500 different masseuses, young and old, a total of 2,000 times, before I realized that massage and boom boom were simply two points in a continuum, just as much as eating and boom boom, or politics and boom boom, or money and boom boom. Boom boom (as the charming natives of Cambodia and some of their neighbours so delightfully and merrily term sex, pronouncing it halfway between boom boom and bum bum) is the sun around which the other planets of human life, such as politics, history, economics, spirituality, trigonometry, art, and yes, massage, revolve.

However, the relationship between massage and boom boom is more than philosophical or theoretical. It is not just that boom boom is simply the farthest and most intimate point in the continuum of touch and human connection that starts with a formal handshake and progresses past a hug, a clothed massage, a minimally clothed massage, a totally unclothed massage, a mutually unclothed massage, a mutually unclothed body-to-body massage, and then on to boom boom, which is arguably the essence of life, the alpha and omega of existence.

In real life, if you were to conduct a sample survey of 20,000 massage establishments the world over, you would realize that in many parts of the world, in the more relaxed and tropical, the Buddhist or Shinto-Confucian countries especially, massage and boom boom are part I and part II, respectively, of an organically connected whole experience. Part I is when the body is kneaded, awakened to life and good health, its circulation improved, its glands beginning to secrete the juices they should be secreting, its pleasure nodes buzzing. And, as these variously aroused parts begin to shake off their former alienation, rebellion, or dysfunctional states and connect with each other, their synergy ignites part II, or the most sacred and most vital act of human existence—fucking.

But a deep and enduring puritanical streak arising from my own West-influenced ideological bent, as well as from the modern Indian civilization in which I was initiated into life, had made me think of massage and sex as totally separate worlds (and there's no better definition of puritanism than H.L. Mencken's 'the haunting fear that someone, somewhere may be happy'). So I would often demand that I be given only massage, unadulterated even by dreams of boom boom. For every improper suggestion or indecent proposal the masseuse made, I mentally deducted 5 per cent from my planned tip.

What a stick-in-the-mud I was then! For at some deep, secret level, all of us pine for the touch of our mothers and our female relatives—touch which was so forthcoming and generous in our childhood, especially in Eastern countries, where children below the age of five, sometimes bare-bottomed, are picked up and cuddled and carried and placed on laps by every woman and prepubescent girl in the vicinity, and consider it their birthright. And oh, the bathing and massage rituals. Sometimes, a woman will combine her bath with that of her child (or the child she is caring for), a kind of intimacy that the child cannot hope to enjoy as it grows up. I have seen, for example, the baby stretched across the naked thighs of a woman who will shortly have her own bath—ah, what a feast of love as the baby inhales the smell of soap and woman, and is enveloped by her warm skin. But this birthright gradually vanishes as the children grow older, and adults and women (if you happen to be male) begin to keep their distance. And the inner child never forgives, and is never reconciled, to the loss.

Thus you are always secretly, and perhaps even unknown to yourself, hungering for that intimate, uninhibited and ungrudging intimacy, and that total and unconditional acceptance. So when you are touched tenderly by a masseuse with soft hands, you are aroused with warm feelings for the whole world, for all of humanity. And if your masseuse, the most immediate, breathing, perfumed and throbbing representative of that humanity, is even passably attractive, your attention gradually turns to her, especially once the major body pains have been taken care of. The nicer she is to you, the nicer you want to be to her, and this feeling sometimes spills beyond the realm of verbal thanks or gifts of cash, goods, coupons or white elephants. It could provoke a desire to respond in kind (in the ultimate example, to return love by making love).

Acknowledging this yearning to touch and to return affection (which was never consummated), one of my best upstate New York masseuses, the soulful and serene Lisa, would always give me a deep hug after I had dressed up and was about to leave.

And yet, sometimes, especially when pain dominates your mind and overpowers all other feelings and thoughts, when unbearable aches or tensions are a stumbling block to daily living and to each moment, or when you don't wish to ruin a long-term professional relationship with the masseuse whose destiny and yours have intersected, you need to pretend to accept this artificial, man-made distinction between massage and sex, simply to avoid being preyed upon for large amounts of cash or being cheated of the therapeutic massage your muscles need. Many a time has a lazy or incompetent masseuse tried to milk me (of my money, and more) by offering a quick sexual climax, often of the hand-assisted variety (and sometimes of the orally assisted variety), hoping thus to escape the hard work that a full therapeutic massage entails. (And, as for escaping the real work of a massage, there are often so-called licenced massage therapists in the US who will try to take time off from working on your body by saying, 'Now breathe.' Just in case you were to *forget* to breathe . . . leaving her with a dead body on her hands.) Rarely, and in my post-marital years, when the formerly therapeutic relationship progressed into mutually enjoyable sex, has it happened that the therapeutic portion deteriorated and shrunk until I was forced to start a long and often painful search for a new masseuse, and to firmly spell out that what I was looking for was 'massage *no* boom boom'—the only unambiguous term that the local taxi drivers, bellboys, guides and touts in Southeast Asia clearly understood—a term that left them little wiggle room for their tricks and surprises.

But trying to keep the massage nonsexual or not openly erotic is easier in certain countries and cultures than in others, and indeed may be easier for Western societies which, like Bill Clinton, are able to rigidly and effortlessly compartmentalize emotions, sex and work. True, in Thailand, there exists a thriving culture of therapeutic traditional Thai massage, supposedly originating from an Indian teacher, where temples double up as massage schools and as places of massage, and this world exists quite apart from the world of sex—or, at least, as far apart as medicine and banking. Respectable family men and women, mothers, fathers and grandmothers get themselves massaged, sometimes in Buddhist temples, or in establishments attached to temples, sometimes in their homes, sometimes on the beach on a blanket or sheet, and sometimes in a studio or salon on tables or mats. These traditional Thai massages are mostly conducted clothed or in loose pyjama-like pants and tops provided by the establishment, and are 100 per cent legitimate (as most prudish Westerners would term them), and are often very cheap—though in private studios and salons they can sometimes get illegitimate and sensual to accommodate your desires, usually for a hefty yet reasonable extra fee. In many other countries, foot massage establishments, a few of them offering other kinds of massage despite their name, are ubiquitous, and invite the weary traveller, tourist or local with their offer of a cheap hour of relaxation and attention, mainly to their feet.

But in other countries, it is relatively harder to find a massage that is purely and nothing but massage. You may discover that the massage you are paying for is a teasing massage designed to make you a horny wreck begging for boom boom or one of its abbreviated relatives. The Thais are masters at this, and the late-arriving Chinese, for whom sixty years of often brutal and godless communism have left them with few religious or moral scruples, are more than a match for them, or so I have heard from tourists returning from the Chinese towns around Shenzen. In a few cases, it is organically and officially 'massage boom boom'—a package deal, take it or leave it, and the *only* item on the menu.

Massage in this part of the world is an aphrodisiac aid to boom boom, a preparation and a provocation for boom boom, the ultimate assertion and expression of life, love and health. I imagine this uncompartmentalized view comes from an earlier and less moralistic time, when kings and princes, faced with a revolt from their underfucked multiple wives, had to be massaged so they could perform again and again, and the prestige, virility and stability of the kingdom ensured, its populace sleeping soundly in the assurance that the royal member was a member in good standing. And why should I condemn these cultures as decadent or inferior for this reason?

It is this journey, from innocence to experience, from a naïve acceptance of my brainwashing by didactic and over-scrupulous American massage therapists to a gradual understanding of my body and the perspectives and practices of massage therapists in less stuck-up parts of the world that I wish to record here. For it is a rich journey—my over three thousand massages were received in over twenty countries around the world, from Canada to Czechoslovakia, from Thailand to Scotland. What's more, I may have seen the only three-nippled masseuse in the world—she showed me her special endowment only after our second session. What it was in me that sparked this special kindness, this intimate sharing, I shall never know, though I do admit trying in a few Asian countries to pick up a bit of the local language. And as I conversed with them like a fellow human being, an equal who was concerned, interested, warm and grateful for their generous touch, they unlocked to me their secrets, one thirty-nine-year-old masseuse suddenly asking me if I could find her a boyfriend.

This journey also includes dozens of real and warm individuals such as Elisa of Long Island. The thing that excites me is that she, a large Romanian who is the furthest possible thing from a romantic prospect because of her plump size and looks and age, is like a mother, with me as her baby. She is like one of those Eastern mothers who are so full of love for their babies that they will kiss and wash every part, every extension, every nook and cranny, as if they are all equally sacred and divine and precious. While they massage you, they own you totally; nothing at all, no inhibition or legal code or provision of New York state law, holds them back. How can I deny the joy of this: of being in my mid-forties, and going back, for a moment, to those blissful few months when I was a baby and completely and unconditionally loved?

That is at least part of the reason why people need massages: they want to feel cared for, touched, babied, accepted and loved unconditionally; they are looking for a refuge from the harsh, unfeeling, uncaring, judging and restrictive world, a world of boundaries fenced with legal barbed wire. God bless these women, and may many more Elisas bloom!

Not just babied, but bathed. One of the most delightful experiences you will ever have, one that is included in the price of some Eastern massages, is being soaped, bathed and towelled dry by your masseuse. In some establishments, as in one Bangalore outfit a few years back, it includes just the act of soaping the unreachable parts of your back (one young Manipuri masseuse named Rosie soaped my front too, but started laughing when she observed the expansive effects, and so did I, rather sheepishly). Whichever, back or front, is a lot better than nothing—as if any woman can trust us inept and gauche men to take proper care of ourselves! Though, reflecting on this experience, I thought later that the ritual may have to do with the masseuses' aesthetic desire not to have to massage a smelly customer.

Also, I have fallen mildly in love with nearly every massage therapist who was good and tender on the table (and therefore, I can almost guarantee, good in bed). Though the more beautiful the massage therapist, the stronger and more passionate the feeling, it has often happened with those who were not primarily pretty in their external appearance, but regal and symphonic in their internal and emotional selves. For a great massage is an act of love, tender and caring, as with the lovely brown-haired Lisa from upstate New York, who has the face, hairstyle and build of a Greek goddess, and who starts softly, her butter-soft hands spreading oil all over my body, and ends by whispering into my ear, 'The massage is finished, thank you', so as not to rudely awaken me. It simply can't be helped; tenderness provokes my fantasy, my loving gratitude.

A good example of this generosity I found one day at a Pennsylvania hotel near Pennsylvania station in midtown New York, where there is a warm and spacious Korean massage spa in which every customer is required to use the sauna and shower before a massage—an effective device, among Japanese and Korean establishments, to get their customers clean and fresh as babies before the massage. This device allows the masseuses to touch you in secret places without any reservations. My masseuse is a Korean woman who turns out to be Christian, in her late forties, at least, probably even half a century. What gentleness and softness. Of course at one point, without provocation or warning, she lifts up my towel and offers a compliment that Dale Carnegie would have approved of. Then, without a cue from me, she starts to kiss, lick and suck my nipple and brush her soft hair against my chest, while her other hand, without the slightest warning, seeks my below-the-waist erogenous zones and whirls about a bit over there. I am surprised and don't know what to do, and am sure I will explode in about sixty seconds, so I exclaim, no, no, stop—and she stops, saying, 'You are a gentleman!' And I laugh, only a semi-hollow laugh. For I am a gentleman indeed, ha ha ha. Well, okay, that's one of my personae (damn!), one of my multiple personalities, but why only acknowledge one?

And then she asks me how many wives I have. Twenty, I say. How about twenty-one, she asks. And to each direction I give her—'Massage here more, please'—she replies, 'Thank you.' She's singing along with the classical muzak oozing from the walls, and stops to ask, 'Can I sing for you?' She doesn't grudge me her femininity, her intimacy, her motherhood. She is too gentle for me to grudge her my high-end tip. For I get a feeling that with each such new soul I meet I am enriched, that it has been my fortune to meet her. And let's face it: there are not that many of them left in this increasingly commercial world. A B-minus rating for the massage, an A-plus rating for her demeanour and humanity.

Indeed, I have had as many different massages as I have had masseuses, because every person brings their special mix of personality, training and temperament to the massage, and these massages have drained my pockets of thousands of dollars, but at least now I have a book: the uncensored confessions of a massage addict, as true and un-whitewashed as James Joyce would have brought you from the deepest recesses of Bloom's blooming brain and Molly's bloomers. And though there are thousands of massage establishments the world over who have a strict policy of massage *no* boom boom—sometimes not the most ideal or intelligent state of affairs—I am thankful even for them (and especially for them), because a world with not enough boom boom would be a much harsher and less bearable place if there was no massage either.

Instead of airdropping bombs and special forces and navy seals on the terrorist-infested areas of the world, thus infuriating the innocent locals by blasting wedding parties to tiny shreds of flesh and hanks of hair and bone—thus breeding more terrorists and recruits for Al Qaeda hell-bent on avenging their vapourized relatives—Bush ought to have dropped special masseuse forces, possibly nicknamed the Pink Berets, on Afghanistan. What a superb massage by a caring, loving woman does is not just drain you of your tension, but drain you of your anger and accumulated resentment towards the world, and even sometimes of a sense of purpose (a bit like the effects of marijuana, which I have too little experience with, except for a few Jamaican brownies and Cambodian 'Happy' Pizzas). Just before the massage, you may have decided you were going to make the Olympics swimming team, become a billionaire, reinvent the wheel, design a better mousetrap, or conquer the world by the age of twenty-five. After a gloriously relaxing massage, you just want to sleep—whether alone, or with a woman. Your ambitions don't seem as important; indeed they don't seem to have any point, for you have become overcome by a feeling of peace and oneness with the world. So the Al Qaeda terrorist will miss boarding the plane he had planned to hijack, and the suicide bomber will say to himself, 'Well, maybe I am still ready to do the deed, but I would first like to enjoy a few more of these massages that I have been missing all my life. Heaven and the promised seventy-two buxom virgins can wait just a while longer.' Consider how, with a bit of kindness and understanding, a handful of masseuses might have changed history and saved hundreds of thousands of innocent lives!

The massages I describe in this book are chiefly about touch, acceptance and tender loving care, and not just about sex. It is most often about pain, and sometimes about sore muscles and large swathes of neglected epidermis seeking their share of attention, fondling, mothering, or tender loving care, because most of the time we are stomachists and penisists and mindists—we vastly favour these three organs while neglecting the rest of our bodies. For example, the underside of the forearm, the back of the knee, the inner thigh, and even the armpit, whose only interest for most people is that they be washed and deodorized—it's almost as if they are pariahs in the caste hierarchy of body parts. In a massage, which is anatomical democracy in action—or should be—they are collecting their democratic due, or at least a portion of their due, for a good massage makes sure that no part of the body is left untouched. Bar none, except, perhaps, the staff of life and its two supporting anchors.

Before I rest my case, a spiritual argument for massage (after all, how could you expect an Indian *not* to be spiritual?). Though I am not religious in the traditional sense, I find myself easily seduced and awed by that blessed state called oneness, wherein we cease to feel the separation or alienation from other human beings which is part of the reason for the world's problems (the other being global warming). And nothing I have known helps to achieve the feeling of oneness more than twoness: a man and a woman coupled in blissful sexual union, or if not sex, at least in a generous and uninhibited massage. And occasionally, threeness, threesomes, or triple massages—but then, I am getting ahead of myself.

Now this is characteristic of a mind inclined towards stream of consciousness, a characteristic that is reflected in this book—the chronological storytelling often pausing for philosophical breaks or digressions or, at times, being abandoned to focus on a specific region or issue.

2

MASSEUSES: GODDESSES AND ASSOCIATE WIVES?

For many years now, especially in monogamously monomaniac, infidelity-despising and Bill Clinton-crucifying America, where to have a reasonably intimate connection with a woman other than your wife is not easy, I have looked upon a good masseuse as nothing less than a goddess. And I don't mean this in the banal, woolly-headed, new age sense of 'Every woman has the goddess in her.' For many years now, I have stopped visiting my regular, born-and-brought-up, parentally indoctrinated church, the Catholic Church. Instead, I now belong to the Church of the Goddess of Massage, at whose temple I worship between two and seven times a week. And each time I receive a blessing, a laying of hands, from one of the better goddesses, like Lisa—soft, accepting, loving, healing, nurturing, enlivening, empowering and sanctifying—I am healed and can face the world with lightness, a smile, a feeling of relaxation and an assurance that life is, after all, worth living. Or at least until the next massage.

To some men, a good masseuse may approach the status of a mistress, a caretaker, and even a wife. For many years I denied that there was a sexual or romantic element in my massages. To be fair, my wife was mostly tolerant and broadminded, not just receiving massages herself—brief ten-minute ones from me, and regular ones from professionals—but also, occasionally, presenting me a massage gift certificate for Christmas or for my birthday, sometimes recommending a particular masseuse by name. However, like one of my later girlfriends, she would sometimes seem jealous, which would make me respond defensively. But now that I have much greater respect for women's remarkable intuition, I realize my ex-wife's jealousy wasn't entirely misplaced, even though I was a lot more self-disciplined and less wild than in my unchained post-marital days (like when my possessive Javanese girlfriend lay in the bed next to mine and watched clueless as the Balinese masseuse, perhaps aroused by a little lust, slyly reached under the towel to probe my hot zones). But I may be a natural polygamist, genetically designed for polygamy-friendly ages and cultures rather than this repressive and humourless monogamous age.

Is massage a form of marriage? Well, try looking up the usual American yellow page directories (which I was often forced to do in the pre-Google era in many a strange city, when desperately in search of a massage). Is it not curious that in many American directories, the 'Massage' listing is sandwiched between 'Marriage Counsellors' and 'Mattresses'? As if to suggest that when you don't spend enough time of your married life doing fun things on a mattress with your spouse, you might end up finding someone else to do fun things on a mattress with. And if you don't (and even if you do find that partner to have fun with), you may then end up consulting a marriage counsellor, while also getting massages to knead out your marital pains, your frustrations, and your hunger for touch.

Thus it has often occurred to me that like geishas—who acted as intimate companions, entertainers and lovers to Japanese men whose wives had stopped giving them the playful and romantic partnership they once did—masseuses may to some extent supplement wives and even perform a healing, supporting role that permits men to remain sane and prevents families from breaking up. But as women of course have sexual needs too, which their husbands may not fully satisfy, they also often need masseuses or masseurs. (Whether or not these masseuses or masseurs become associate husbands, I leave a woman theorist with the appropriate Harvard, Brown, Berkeley or Princeton advanced degree to decide.) For there are bound to be women who feel that their husbands don't touch them enough, don't pay enough attention to all parts of their bodies, and who go for the main thing—that sacred and magical area between a woman's thighs—too quickly and come too soon, after which, according to many stand-up comediennes, they instantly turn over and start snoring. Their bodies suffer from a deep hunger that needs more loving care which, in the absence of a *Kamasutra*-savvy lover, may need to be provided for by a masseuse or a masseur.

In any case, I have no doubt that sexual frustration and bad marriages (or periodically stormy marriages like mine), which like death and taxes will always be with us, are part of the reason why people need massages. To pretend that the two are totally unrelated is so unrealistic that a masseuse who thinks thus deserves to be debarred from the profession for being so clueless about her subjects and about human psychology.

If you doubt the comparison of massage to marriage, take this test: How many of you have been touched by your spouses, gently, unhurriedly and erotically on your underarms, flanks, back of knees, behind the ears, toes, on the crease between the buttock and the thigh, and every square inch, crease and fold of your pelvic region, especially those hidden creases nestling between your thighs? Ninety per cent of men are touched on fewer parts of their bodies by their wives than they are by their massage therapists (and to be fair to wives, many of them have jobs and lead far too stressful lives to give their and their husbands' bodies their just due, thus requiring specialist intervention). Indeed, a talented masseuse can arouse and awaken erogenous zones or parts of you whose existence your wife never knew of, which even you didn't know of, which in fact didn't exist until your masseuse brought them into existence. And once awakened, you are left yearning and completely at her mercy for the next few massages. Indeed, on more than one occasion, a masseuse has pointed out to me a bump or cut or some other damage to my body that I was unaware of, perhaps in the nick of time before it grew into a malignant tumour or a more serious problem.

Oh sure, I had real pains all the time—98 per cent of the time, except when returning for a quick second or third massage by a beautiful masseuse I had become a little enchanted with in my later, lonelier, less-loved years. Tightness in my shoulders and arms from bending for long hours over a laptop, fibromyalgia, myofascial pain, chronic fatigue, pains in my feet, thighs and buttocks, some owing to flat feet and a podiatric racket in which rock-hard inserts would be prescribed as a corrective, inserts whose steepness and hardness caused pain to radiate all over my body. I tried regular physical therapy, which mildly strengthened my back, but was no substitute for massage, just as a pop melody or jingle is no substitute for a Mozart symphony. But which came first: the body ache or the marital pain, the feeling of being insufficiently loved, cared for, worshipped and touched? A question not easily answered, but worth researching with Kinsey-like integrity and labour, unless we're simply aching for quick, convenient and moralistic answers to match our prejudices. Besides, in the first fifteen years of my marriage, I was blessed with a far greater libido than could be satisfied by my 3–5 times a week lovemaking sessions with my wife; some of that excess sexual energy could have surfaced as a yearning for massage, when I could be legally touched by women other than my wife.

So massage is an unrecognized form of marriage, except that in massage, polygamy and polyandry are tolerated and often encouraged, and homosexual marriages are as legal as heterosexual ones. Or else, there are monogamous interludes sandwiched between occasional affairs, and sometimes, a promiscuous run of one-afternoon stands. You may use a separate masseuse every day of your life, or have two or three masseuses work on your body simultaneously—and no one except perhaps the Pope or your Victorian spinster aunt is gonna regard it as anything but a therapeutic quest at best, and as delicious and wholesome fun at worst, as harmless an eccentricity as eating your Big Mac in a different McDonalds each day of your life. Because a large number of the planet's residents, emerging from a darker and repressive age, have entered a more permissive, sensual and liberated age. This book is meant to celebrate this happy development and furnish you with ideas on how to fulfil and spice your dreams—and that of your lover, wife or husband . . . and of their lovers and masseuses. And perhaps those of their mothers and their aunts.

PART II

WESTERN MASSAGE: FROM NUDE TO BLANKETED

3

WHOLESOME AND HOLISTIC MASSAGES IN AMERICA

On a cloudy autumn day, in a middle-class neighbourhood of Murray Hill close to the Midtown Tunnel and marked by monotonous brownstone apartment buildings, I was introduced to my second American masseuse, Janet—thirty-fivish, dark-haired, and operating out of the Manhattan studio that was also her home. Janet not only didn't offer me a towel, but simply said, 'Take off *all* your clothes and lie on the table', pointing to the centre of the room.

Around this time, my wife, I and our little son had moved to a large home set in a one-acre garden in the Long Island suburbs, but I still regularly visited Manhattan for theatre, art movies at the Film Forum and Lincoln Center, bookstores, readings, and the hipster, young and artistic atmosphere of Greenwich Village, the East Village and Soho. Now I had an additional reason: massage, which was fifty times more easily available, and with far greater diversity, than in Long Island. Janet had ten years of experience, a Siamese cat, and an apartment strewn with cat hair and cat toys. A painted portrait of her younger self suggested she had once been quite a hottie, and a beauty besides, though now she seemed rather mellow in comparison, dressed in a blue-collar faded jeans and a jacket, buttons opened to flash her ample cleavage.

I did as directed, though I had such an instant erection, the result of my excitement at this novel experience, that I had difficulty wriggling out of my tight jeans. When I did, I lay on the table nude with a monstrous erection whose existence she took no notice of. It was a strange and puzzling experience: to have a woman observe my aroused naked body, my pole pointing at the sky, and not seem to feel, think or say a thing. So each time I would think of getting a massage from her—I could be at home, or on the train from Long Island to the city—I would have an erection or a trouser smile that would last at least for a few minutes until something else, say the gruff voice of a ticket collector, distracted my thoughts.

Janet applied oil to and massaged every part of me except the sex organs themselves, and her massages had a completeness that many others could not give. If a masseuse was good, I didn't care if she covered me with ten blankets, so long as I could still breathe, and when the time came, she attended to each and every part that needed therapeutic attention (excepting the Big One and his little twin brothers). But once I got used to Janet's open-air policy, any incompetent masseuse enforcing modesty with a heavy hand would leave me feeling cheated.

It also helped that Janet really liked my friends A. Ductor and G. Luteus Maxim—who happen, coincidentally, to be friends of Al Gore too, if his accuser Molly is to be believed. (Meaning, she spent a considerable length of time massaging my (and Al Gore's) favourite muscles: the adductor muscles (inner thighs) and the gluteus maximus muscles (butt, buttocks, bottom cheeks). Favourite, because thanks to my painful podiatric inserts, they were both highly sensuous yet ache-filled areas for me. You can use your imagination to guess what happened, or else I'll tell you later in the book.

These were immensely stressful times for me, both personally and professionally. And though my loving wife and my three lovely children—two chubby, fun-filled toddlers, and my nine-year-old computer assistant—

helped offset some of it, massages became absolutely essential to unblock the tension and the soreness; without them I couldn't even think, let alone write.

However, despite lusting in my heart after Manhattan's legions of lovely women, and freely admitting it in my writings, my massages, having begun in therapeutic wholeness and in medical necessity, remained thus; for many years, I was sanctimonious about the completely 'therapeutic' nature of the massage I wanted.

But around 1995, I ran into a Russian immigrant masseuse named Ella—sweet, warm, quite pretty, and besides, earthy—the kind who makes your sanctimoniousness melt away in about thirty seconds. While massaging me in a midtown studio run by a shrewd Korean businesswoman, who screened her visitors with the help of a buzzer and a security camera, Ella noticed that I had a boner which had made a tent of the brief towel, and that it was causing me anxiety because of my embarrassment and my unsuccessful attempt to hide it. She asked if she could 'take care' of it for me. With automatic and pompous sanctimoniousness I said, 'No, I prefer to keep my massage for therapeutic relief and relaxation, and to have my erotic needs attended to by my wife.'

Said she: 'There's no way this massage is going to relax you so long as you have that.'

I saw her point, and the absurdity of my rigid 'stand'; it was as if a 1,000-watt light bulb had suddenly lit up in my brain. And most of all, I appreciated her concern and her naturalness, and began to realize that the word 'therapeutic' need not be restricted to just certain parts of the body—that even the body believes in equality and equal rights, and despises discrimination between its various parts.

I now believe that in some cases, helping a male client ejaculate may be an essential part of the massage process, because any bottled-up sexual tension inhibits the very relaxation the massage is designed to effect. But I also equally support the right of the masseuse to choose *not* to do it. Besides which, I myself almost never ask for it or even *allow* it, surrendering only very rarely to offers I cannot refuse. Why?

Partly because my surplus mojo would sometimes burst through the emergency door and leak out without any specific intervention, and sometimes without my even wanting it to. But also partly because an extortionate mindset often takes over many masseuses the moment they think they have an erect penis and, by extension, a captive prisoner. In certain Asian countries, for just the work of five minutes it takes her to make you ejaculate, a masseuse might demand double or triple the price of the massage itself. Because she has you by the balls, to speak metaphorically (and with some Thai masseuses, literally so, for they don't believe in using light artillery when they can bring in the heavy one right away and achieve their objective!). But I will explain my personal choices in greater detail later.

After meeting Ella, however, I gradually gave up my humourless moral objections and self-duping mind games. And when I found a masseuse who was affectionate towards me, relaxed and not extortionate, I relaxed my own attitude. As with Kristina, a masseuse who was so comfortable and relaxed with my body and with me that she would spread my legs one foot apart and massage almost every place she could find between them with perfect ease and naturalness and love, and would then turn me around and pick up my penis without my permission, as if she owned it, as if she had every goddamn right in the world. I was so surprised and grateful for the trust implied in this gesture that I let her do what she would, what she almost *wanted* to do. By now, and this was around 1999, I had discovered that life and love were fragile things, and that life was too short for me to affect a holier-than-thou attitude and say, 'No, I don't want *pleasure*. I am too noble and virtuous to be tempted by mere pleasure. I want only a *massage*, thank you!'

Or the plump Romanian masseuse Elisa, who I rate a 9 on 10. If there's one masseuse who can give competition to any massage therapist, it is Elisa. She goes straight for your tits. Hers is that perfect combination of pleasure, therapeutic relief, nurturing, erotic ecstasy, teasing and frustration, and innocence; she is the perfect counterargument to anyone who argues that masseuses are just of two types: legitimate and illegitimate. Hers is the eroticism of the unknown, the mysterious, the ambiguous, and the unexpected.

Her soft fingers graze your perineum when they travel up your thighs, and no matter what she's doing when she's engaged with the middle four-fifths of your body, she is brushing up against your rampant or slightly subdued penis. Her fingers are soft, her face is a combination of mischief and childish playfulness. 'Who, me?' her expression seems to say, as she accidentally—oops, sorry!—squeezes the joy juice out of you.

I met Elisa around 1998 when my marriage was unravelling, and the extra stress needed extra comforting. However, I will also admit that in my earlier, pompously righteous and holier-than-thou years, there were two accidents.

The first was with Janet, my regular masseuse for twelve years. On my second visit, without even asking me, she simply picked up my cock, which had been erect throughout the massage, and started moving her hands up and down on it, having applied some oil to her hands. This was so new for me, it being twenty years before I would hear of lingam massage (the sophisticated cousin of the lowly dick massage), that I didn't object, but just watched in fascination, as if hypnotized by her movements. And as I had already been aroused for a full hour, it didn't take me too long to come.

However, Janet was so mechanical and clinical about it that I regarded hers as a purely medical intervention, or as an artist's experiment in the pursuit of his art. But as I was morally ambivalent about this and didn't tip her, or even say 'Thanks for lending a helping hand to my little monster', the 'accident' was never repeated.

The second accident happened at a semi-upscale Murray Hill joint catering to a yuppie hedonistic and me-generation clientele. Janet being busy that day, I was desperately calling up numbers from *The Village Voice* and then from the *New York* magazine, and discovered one place that had an immediate opening at 2 p.m.

At this well-decorated spa with plants and a fish tank, I was shown to a room and asked to strip fully, lie on the table face up, and await my masseuse.

I did as told, and as there was no towel, and the mystery of who my masseuse might be excited me, I was fully erect even before anyone had even touched me. Then a gorgeous young mulatto woman, either Caribbean or Brazilian, perhaps twenty-two, with a sweet smiling face and a spectacular body, came in, saw what was on the table, and decided to seize the day (had she watched the movie *Seize the Day* I wondered later). She slipped out of her clothes within seconds and, with not a word exchanged, easily and expertly, with her juicy and nearly hairless vagina, mounted my fully perpendicular tool! I was astonished, for it was like a goddess descending from the heavens in answer to my prayers—too stunned to say anything, and too ecstatic at my luck to register my procedural or philosophical objections (or perhaps I had been sedated by the tranquillizers I was then taking). Squatting over me, she slid up and down, and up and down, smooth as a pole dancer, and with a mix of such tenderness, enthusiasm and pure lust that, it being one of my rare extramarital experiences as well as perhaps my only extramarital woman-on-top experience, I might have ejaculated quickly. However, I was barely forty years old and virile, having recently sired three sons one after another, and had this biological quirk that in the mornings and afternoons, unlike evenings and nights, it could sometimes take me forever to come, even to the point of frustration; so I wasn't about to ejaculate quickly.

But just five minutes into this dream, a female supervisor burst into the room, observed the proceedings with shock, and exclaimed, 'No, no! Not *him*!' And instantly, my mulatto lover climbed off my disappointed pole and with a shy smile, hurried into her clothes and out of the room.

Then, slowly, I got it. Besides giving regular massages, this place was also a cover for a high-class brothel, and I was not to be fucked, because I hadn't paid for sex. I was paying seventy dollars for the hour, and not even in your wildest fantasies could you have sex with a beautiful young woman in New York City for less than double that figure, if not quadruple.

I now guess my accidental lover had been a newcomer, and recall with nostalgia that innocent time when one could still think of fucking without a condom—I mean, the AIDS scare had gotten around quite a bit, but some of us still believed that the disease struck mainly gays and drug addicts, and were willing to take our chances. But wait a moment, stop! The AIDS issue is a pure afterthought—a retrospective comment inserted as I write this many years later. At that particular moment, I was in a dream, as in a terrific sexual dream which you simply don't want to end even though you half-know it is reality, so all I did was lie there passively watching her slide up and down my cock with the lithe grace of a dancer while my heart thumped with joy. The morbid fear of disease is a luxury of the super-haves, not of someone for whom it was the first such occurrence.

Given the magnitude of my loss (my cosmic but subsonic shout, 'Oh, shit!' was recorded in a faraway galaxy), my memory has deleted what happened after that (my guess is they sent in a substitute to give me a regular massage)—because in those days, as I was still married, and mainly quite happily too, I had to write these truly rare incidents down in a secret diary and hope they wouldn't be discovered. What else was I going to do? Sobbingly confess to my still most beloved and precious wife that for a few heavenly minutes I had been the victim of an ambush, of a vicious assault by a suddenly descending and gorgeous vagina?

4

EURO-LIBERATED MASSAGE

A year or two after I had been introduced to Janet, I would frequently visit a New Hampshire Writers Colony in the picture-postcard village of Contoocook, near Concord. Here, a horribly crooked bed and mattress, possibly designed for a hunchback, loaded my back and neck with intense bad-mattress pain, which had its corresponding near-ecstatic counterpoint: massage (which is so much more breathtakingly relieving and joyous when your body is in real bad shape, as if the pleasure were directly proportional to the pain you started with). The engine of my relief this time: Jacqueline. A lean blonde with a French accent and a tight body, mostly wrapped in a black body suit like a modern dancer's, she had massaged me earlier at the multi-masseused and hang-loose new age spa Earthstar. Earthstar had a pool where nude coed swimming was permitted, and that was where I had seen my first ever sun-kissed pudenda and learnt the lesson that in any massage joint with no hang-ups about the body, the massages are likely to be fantastic, or at least three notches above the ones elsewhere—because there is a direct relationship between discomfort with the naked human body and bad massages . . . which is why a month in a nudist colony should be an essential part of every masseuse's training.

Jacqueline now worked independently from her humble three-bedroom ranch home in a village not far from New Hampshire's capital, Concord. She doesn't have any towel pretences, for she belongs to the Gallic-German natural-is-best school. Her hands caress and pull apart buttocks as if she were a prison guard checking for concealed drugs while copping a free look, and she forcibly separates your legs. I want to say, 'Ouch, stop it, that's as far as they will go', but she does it anyway to form an acute angle, which the penis is meant to bisect into two nearly equal angles—possibly a female geometry professor's delight while teaching a class of equally delighted girl students. I envy her for the aerial view she must have of my long, lean and tight body, a view which I myself am denied. Her hands travel right up to my groin to embrace my whole thigh, so that not a square millimetre is left unmassaged.

By now I have had, almost by accident, a few sublimely erotic massages with mostly European masseuses—many of these at the St. James Club for health and fitness in London—whose massages were almost better than the best sex, and who combined personal charm, tenderness, magical fingers and perhaps a pinch of concealed lust or mischief to produce an erotic symphony of all the senses. Such women betrayed not a flicker of guilt about the word 'sex', and abounded in playfulness; yet, to use the word 'sex massage' to describe their work would be about as vulgar as to use the word 'broad' to describe Isabella Rossellini.

Jacqueline's overall massage is a sensuous symphony, so rhythmic and concert-like, like a religious ritual, like high church, with the music of Bach playing in the background. The way she circles her hands around your buttocks, separating the cheeks slightly. And her back-of-the-thigh massage, which moves in a parabolic curve from the back of the knee to the inner thigh, finger-flicking those sensitive adductors, lightly feather-dusting the groin and balls and working its way up to where the front of your thigh joins the belly. And the way she spreads your legs, when working on your back, so that her view of your vitals is a grandstand one, the tip of the rosy penis emerging out at full mast, like an exclamation mark, from under your balls. I assign her massage a rating of 7 in general and 9.5 for its sensuality.

'You are breathing well,' she says, responding to my deep breathing.

'It's an automatic reaction whenever a massage is getting to my real sore areas,' I reply. 'When I'm breathing well, it means your massage is good.'

She laughs and pecks a kiss on my forehead.

And that's as far as it goes (or went), unfortunately. Though I was aroused to the point of madness, we never fucked, perhaps because I was too tongue-tied to take the initiative. Born an orphan, raised by nuns for fifteen years, and then after a brief marriage, raising her children alone for twenty years. Pain and loneliness have tightened her face and drained her emotions; so she uses hands, her only permissible tools for expression, and sends super-erotic messages out into the universe through them.

Should I have confessed my weakness, my tendency to fall in love with good masseuses, my love born of gratitude, pouring in from a million pleasure sensors spread throughout my epidermis? A couple of corny seduction speeches, thankfully never delivered, ran through my mind:

> Don't you know that your touch is so erotic that after a while I lose all consciousness that you are separate from me, that I am the massaged and you the masseuse? There I am, spread out before you, totally in your power, trusting your fingers, trusting your touch. When you touch me, I am charged by your electricity, and then I charge others, if I can, though that's not so easy in this rubber-gloved society, in which we are robots acting out the instructions or scripts given to us by television or popular culture . . .
>
> True, I am married and have a beautiful wife. But at this moment, I feel nearly dead, needy, tired, sleepy and vaguely horny, and all I know is that we are born, we screw around, we die, and then we become worm food, never to be heard from again. Would it be such a bad thing if, before the worms get us, we made love just once?

None of this was ever spoken, however. (Besides which, I know now, women are seduced not with speeches, but with subtle X factors including body language, the right cologne, and the right Wall Street trader job, or a billion in the bank and a nifty collection of whips.) So I had my massages, received the occasional virginally pure hug or mommy-like pecked kiss, paid her fee, and rode off into the sunset and back to my room with the horrid bed.

5

THE WALL STREET TANTRIC MASSAGE AND THE FINNISH PUSSYCAT

Manhattan, the capital of the world, a city packed with the top talents in every field, from neurosurgery to bondage, from literature to gastronomy, is also home to some awful pretenders and snake oil salesmen. This capital of the world attracts world-class conmen and -women, some of whom pass themselves off as spiritual leaders and healers, and advertise their dubious offerings to the credulous in new age publications such as the *Whole Life Times*—to which I have myself fallen victim more than once.

Ah, yes. It is an age in which any two-bit twerp who recently operated a hot dog stand in a corn-pone town thinks that holding his or her hands in the air above some pathetic sucker and saying 'Breathe deeply' or 'Feel the spirit!' makes him or her a healer. A healer, and therefore a (Cabinet) Minister of Universal Energy, who must be paid with reverence and universally acceptable hard cash (they don't mind if you go easy on the reverence, but the hard cash is non-negotiable). And everyone who comes to these healers is, by definition, sick, guilty, inferior, a retard who must be condescended to and told things like, 'You may keep your underwear on' (and sometimes, 'you may keep your radiation-proof body suit on').

But one adventurous afternoon in the late nineties—by now, my published novel had received considerable acclaim and I felt more confident—I boarded a train to Penn Station and then took the subway to Wall Street, emerging into a street that was a canyon in the skyscraper section of downtown New York, and not far from the Twin Towers. I entered one of these skyscrapers, and went in for an experience that had all the hallmarks of the good old-fashioned American sucker story. And yet, it had enough novelty, mystery, open-mindedness and excitement for me to justify at least a portion of the hundred bucks I shelled out.

It was a 'tantric massage' administered by a Russian woman and man, between twenty-nine and thirty-five, both looking immensely sharp, like KGB double agents, this being a time when post-Soviet Russians had invaded New York City and were buying up real estate, spas and hair salons. The setting: a Wall Street office room decorated with pictures of an Indian guru facing a Christian cross, candles and a chalice, incense sticks spreading a sandalwood perfume through the room's heated air. After undressing behind a partition, I was instructed to enter the room naked, which I did, preceded by my full-mast flagpole, and watched by two pairs of eyes. As directed, I lay down on a mattress on the floor, and was subjected to a synchronized massage by a pair of female hands on my left side and a pair of male hands on my right. My male chauvinist consciousness tried to concentrate on the soft female half of the touch (and the fact that she, yippie!, briefly brushed her finger against my pee-pee). The so-called tantric massage ended with a 'prostate massage'—a massage of dick, balls and perineum simultaneously—which, finally, made me ejaculate in full view, as the tantrics had desired (and why would I wish to disappoint them?). It was my most spiritual and public coming ever, and I wonder now if there was a secret camera recording these proceedings for history or for prying eyes—and, if so, if I could buy the rights for the film.

Anyway, once I had cleaned myself up and dressed, I was allowed to ask questions of the master. I could say the name of a woman and I would be told what kind of sexual relations I could expect with her. Having just had an emission, thanks mainly to the woman's probing fingers, I was a little dazed; my memory cells were out in the streets partying and celebrating my good luck.

When you think about it (and I mustn't be too unkind, for I don't quite know the relative percentages of their actual knowledge and charlatanry), it was hilarious: the author of a well-known, sexually liberated book receiving sexual advice from a pair of charlatans. Still, I didn't want to miss out on some fun, especially as I had paid for it and, as a writer, had a certain licence in these things. He can pretend and probe and go with the flow, because ultimately he'll turn every damn thing, every shit big and small, into literary material.

I said, 'Luba.'

'Oh, a Russian girl? Well, she hasn't had much good sex in her life, so what she needs is not sensitivity, but hard fucking. A good strong dick. She could potentially really go for you.'

I said, 'Sheila.'

'Sheila, she is good, but she has another man that she might be interested in.'

'What about my sexual future?'

'You will reach your peak in 2–3 years. Then you will have lots of women and pleasure. At fifty-one, you will start losing interest in physical sex; women will come to you more for play and fun than for your fucking.'

'Am I average or above average?' I asked.

'You are well above average. And if you only do the exercises that contract your prostate without tensing your buttocks and legs, you'll be able to control the length of your erection tremendously.

'Sex is very important to you. You think a lot about it. It is okay to think about it, but don't worry about it, and it will come to you. *Women, they need to feel that you are cool and relaxed. They can sense tension and worry. If you are relaxed, they'll come to you.*'

I had to admit that these sounded like words of wisdom, besides which in three out of four specific answers to my questions, their judgement had been uncannily accurate. To have the relaxed attitude to life—that itself was worth perhaps 500 bucks, or five times what I had paid. Though, despite his prediction, post-fifty-one I am still interested in sex, and though there has not exactly been legions of women, yet, in their defence I can say that they were probably waiting for me to have the relaxed attitude to life.

Immigrants, the lifeblood of America, and the chief reason for its vitality, creativity and continuous reinvention of itself, had begun to revitalize New York's massage scene in the nineties. While Russians entered it in the early nineties, their hallmarks being technical proficiency, nonchalance about naked bodies, and giving a decent butt massage, the Koreans entering in the latter half were juicy Lucys, often arousing the men until they begged for some relief. And while stray Koreans like Jeannie could be extremely good, Korean masseuses are generally more expensive and expect large tips, so I only used them when my regular masseuses were unavailable.

It's a grey and drizzly late Autumn day in Manhattan, a day in which one massage appointment after another turns bad. And then, suddenly, it turns out that the rejections and failures are the best thing to have happened to me. For the next number I call yields a warm 'Yes, I can give you an appointment right now.' And twenty minutes later, I meet the most glorious Finnish girl I have ever come across, and spend the best eight-five dollars of my life.

Her name, she tells me, is Tessa. She is around 5'9", but looks taller, because she wears high heels. She has light blonde hair.

The room is lit with candles and a soft table lamp, and perfumed by incense. To my surprise, she asks me to get naked.

'Not many people come here who are as horny as you,' she says, smiling, as I drop my pants, revealing a flagpole at a 90-degree angle to my legs.

Her sweet nature matches her voice on the phone; what's more, to my surprise, she strips and performs the massage in the buff, with not even a toe-ring or a bracelet on her. The vision will stay with me forever: of glorious, pert, pink-nippled breasts and a pussy with only a faint fuzz of golden hair—a curvaceous body to die for. The face of a goddess: high cheekbones, blue eyes, blonde hair, classic beauty. Like a *Playboy* centrefold, like one of the women from the movie *Caligula*.

Is it a dream? She even spreads her pussy's lips to show me her inner sanctum—those ruby-coloured inner lips. It is absolutely weird, the architecture of the moment: to be domed, not by the Sistine Chapel ceiling, or my childhood's thatched fake roof that was a home for rats, but by a glorious golden pussy, so to speak. And, surprise, surprise! She feels not an ounce of shame about exposing her body thus.

She also lets her well-oiled breasts trace circles of various parabolic shapes on my chest and belly clockwise, then anticlockwise.

The variety of techniques surprises me. Rubbing her breasts against various parts of my body, drawing her hair over my back and buttocks making every pore come tinglingly alive, applying oil to her breasts, then massaging my penis with them.

At one point, while her mouth is occupied with delivering doses of ecstasy to my lower half, her vulva is directly above my face, and it looks so clean, golden and delicious, and her body emits such a rapturous scent, that my tongue, almost as if it has a mind of its own, leaps out of my mouth and starts to lick the butter-soft lips dangling above me, like grapes at some Roman orgy—one of the few times I have ever licked a woman's cunt—and is rewarded with pure vaginal nectar.

At one point, she cradles each of my hands and then each of my feet in the warmth of her vulva while she is busy massaging the upper part of my leg or arm . . . I can't believe my luck: all I had expected was a competent massage.

So what's the catch?

It seems there's none. She is just a genuinely nice and sensual person from one of the freest countries in the world. Maybe I will write her story, I say to her effusively. Her massage is completely unimportant to me; she is. My dormant romantic, passionate self had been aroused.

I ask her when she had come to America.

'Six weeks back,' she replies.

'That explains it,' I say. 'Sad to say, you'll change.'

In a moment of wild fantasy, I want to get this Finnish masseuse for myself before someone else gets her, and she loses her freshness and vitality. I am even willing to go to Finland and get lost in there. No, why complicate things? I want to meet her after the massage and make her my lover.

I am exultant, I feel different.

'Where have you been all my life?' I blurt out—a phrase I have never, ever before uttered in real life, being merely a corny line I had heard in some movie. And now it just burst out of me, spontaneously.

After the massage, Tessa treats me with special kindness and respect because I am a writer, a published author—something I noticed in the Russians, Czechs and Finns I met at the time, most of whom were well-read, and had a pretty much universal and profound reverence for writers, and who were less likely to respond with dispiriting comments such as 'A writer? Oh, written any bestsellers?' or, 'I have an idea for a book—will you write it for me?'

She also tells me later that there can be no actual sex, for she has a boyfriend. Smitten and greedily hoping to graduate to real sex, I had made the mistake of telling her I loved her.

Later, I realized that it was more in the sexual intimacy we had reached, and in the rapture I felt at the sweetness of her person, that I felt something like love for her—a love mingled with gratitude and awe. But I didn't explain all this, and had simply said, 'I love you'—as if this might earn me a promotion to fourth base.

Bad move. For she was one of those literal women who responded that since she had a boyfriend, and as I had used the word love, she couldn't see me anymore. To think that it was my only experience until then with someone with the exquisite body of a blonde Penthouse centrefold, fully waxed or naturally hair-disadvantaged, with a generously large and swollen-lipped, silky smooth vulva—and I had blown it?

Later, I understood her highly liberal, yet Western and compartmentalized thought process: she had promised her boyfriend that she would be selling erotic services, but not love. Eroticism, pure and unadulterated, had been distilled from the rather viscous mix that it is part of, in real life—and this pure eroticism could be marketed in capitalistic McBites or occasional Whoppers, with a little philanthropic service thrown in. I am flattered that she thought my love real enough—and I wondered if she perhaps felt some herself too.

Meanwhile, there would be no other massage in this league until I began my post-divorce visits to Southeast Asia.

6

THE TROUBLE WITH MEN AND MEN

Scene: Miami Beach, 1999. The long strip of beach, residences, motels, hotels and restaurants starting from above South Beach, running up through middle-class and posh neighbourhoods like Bal Harbour, and then past the nudist Haulover Beach and to the Sunny Isles section, lined with endless condos, hotels and motels, was my home for the first three months of 1999. I was here fleeing domestic disharmony and trying to finish a book-in-progress, and for a month I lived in a middlebrow motel room with a view of the beach. And sometimes, I needed to call in a male massage therapist because the women seemed to be busier and more expensive.

On one such day, when the masseuses seemed to be either busy or hiding behind their answering machines, I call a guy named Jay, who could not come (no pun or offence meant, but I do have this slight apprehension that a male massage therapist might be gay and, in the privacy of my room, lose self-control and . . .). I mean Jay was too busy to come, so he put me on to his staff sergeant (just kidding!), Mike, who arrived at my door soon thereafter.

From the Miami *New Times* it was evident that men seemed to go for a song: a 1.25 hour massage from Robert Allen, therapist at the Atlanta

Olympic Games, cost only $40. Imagine that! For forty bucks, you wouldn't get even a blind, one-armed masseuse in America! (Speaking of blind masseuses, I remember running all the way around Chiang Mai in Thailand searching for the blind masseuse joint, for it gave me such a kick to imagine the masseuse accidentally stumbling onto my third leg or the misplaced cucumber—'Oops, so sorry!' 'No problem, help yourself! And while you're at it, why not have a ball?') Women could command such high fees because they were favoured both by men (the pigs!) and also by other women, feminists especially (oh, the piggies!).

Mike's fee was $35 for the hour, and he came to your door, which meant you didn't have to drive through stop-and-start Miami Beach traffic, a mishmash of senior citizens and drug dealers, and find a parking spot—a steal of a deal, and sensible, because of my strained finances. With Puerto Rican or Cuban looks, this medium-built man had a slightly pudgy face and mildly wavy hair. Though I was apprehensive and defensive, evading his eyes and keeping my towel firmly in place over my member to forestall any misplaced conclusions or stumbles, he ended up giving me a fairly proficient massage. While leaving he said, 'It was a *pleasure* to massage you.' And I thought: 'I hope you don't really mean it. Or else, I will be forced to fire you. Or, at the very least, to charge you for your pleasure.'

I called him again, two days later. Besides being a lot cheaper than women, he was a no-hassle guy, always available, grateful, appearing at your door within one and a half hours of your phoning him.

Anyway, I decided to be a bit more free-tongued that day, an investigative journalist. How did he deal with his female massage subjects and their bodies? I asked. 'Some of them *insist* on *not* being covered. Then I just ask to turn down the lights.' Strange, that he preferred not to look at these women who wanted to air their assets; in his place, I might have asked, 'Can I turn on *all* the lights? Please? And bring my camera along the next time?' And though I didn't ask if he was gay, I decided to bring matters a little out into the open—figuratively speaking, of course (I thought talking about it might solve the problem—the Sigmund Freud fallacy that I still hadn't completely abandoned at the time)—by saying, 'I am embarrassed that I sometimes get erections during a massage.' He said half the men he massaged got erections. Hearing this, I felt mightily relieved and a little relaxed for a while. Even my dick took a mini-break.

But as he massaged my chest, he avoided touching my nipples and I, burning with nipple neglect, spoke thus: 'Hey, Bud, what about them poor little buds?!' No joking, I actually said something more cunning such as, 'Could you go crosswise from the shoulder downwards?' demonstrating with a flat hand moving over my chest. Because hey, man, the perimeter is a mental perimeter, and life is short—so fuck perimeters, parking metres and talking metres.

So he did, and a good and nearly sexy and soothing chest and stomach massage it was, his hands stroking the sides of my trunk and reaching slightly underneath.

At which point the trouble started. For it didn't matter, male or female—in those days, I would either way get an erection when touched in erogenous zones like the thighs, buttocks, nipples or lower abdomen, and sometimes the flanks of my trunk (although, unlike a man, a woman with soft hands could touch even my hands and give me a hard-on—sometimes even the mere expectation of a woman touching me might give me a hard-on). The erection embarrassed me, but I somehow dealt with it, because massage is like medical treatment—the relief of pain is the foremost goal, and you are not going to stop yourself from going to doctors just because they make you wear those silly open-butt gowns and perform painful prostate examinations, are you? But still, I was terrified of an accidental ejaculation, and wished to ask him how other straight men handle such situations. But I didn't.

Once again, when he started to massage my infamous right leg and his touch included my penis, though sideways and 'accidental', it caused my peepee to metamorphose again into something greater than itself. And later, when he lifted both my legs trying to bring my feet and knees up in a stretch towards my chest, a full erection rose like a flagpole. The erection and the leg stretch conspired together to dislodge the towel, which fell off my body and I didn't replace it, leaving my cock standing just like that. (I silently lectured myself that I must overcome this 'embarrassment' about natural things like my body and bodily phenomena, having just talked to him about it, and besides, I was mildly curious to see what might happen—even though I wouldn't be cool enough to handle a joking 'Oh, so you *are* rather glad to see me, are you?')

I now realized the stiffy must have been a provocation, if he was indeed gay. For having made forays towards my pubic boundary while massaging my stomach, he suddenly brushed my penis with his hand as if casually and accidentally, and when I did not object to that initial movement, if indeed it was accidental, he went on to give a single, unequivocal stroke. At which point, even before the conclusion of his first downward stroke, with split-second speed, I stopped him with, 'I am not looking for that!' Later, I was so embarrassed and angry with myself (and him), thinking, *God, how could I have allowed myself to get into such a situation?*

So that was as far as anything went with my male massage therapists in America. Though there could have been a few undercover emissions, because when lying face down, one cannot react quickly enough to stop a stroke that is too arousing. And while touch is not always gender-neutral—sex being nearly all in the mind—it *sometimes* is, especially if the male therapist has soft hands.

Luckily, the incident with Mike happened late in my American experience, and in a hotel room—hotel rooms are notorious for inspiring impure thoughts, can't blame anyone. An Indian friend of mine used to assert that if you placed a healthy man and woman together in a room, and both were sure that no one else would ever find out, they would sooner or later end up fucking. Regardless of the truth of his theory (despite him being a very fine long-term friend, he also happened to be a horny Keralite, suggesting that the theory ought to be ingested with a tiny pinch of salt), the potential for such embarrassing situations partly explains why, for sixteen years of getting regular massages in America, even in health clubs like Jack La Lanne, I always preferred a masseuse to a masseur—when available. Blame my genes and my upbringing, if you like—but barring a real handshake, a hand on the shoulder, a hug from a close friend or from a European from the demonstrative Latin countries, and one awesome masseur at the Bally's Hotel in Atlantic City, I am not fully relaxed about a man touching my body (nor would I bend to pick up a fallen piece of soap in a Greek bathhouse). And a massage is one place where I want to feel relaxed enough that it would be okay, even nice, if I drift off to sleep while it is in progress. Is this too much to ask for—to feel comfortable during a massage I am paying through my nose for? But even when forced to choose a masseur, I try to avoid the he-man types who treat their male subjects' bodies roughly, as if fearful that some tenderness or softness may signal homosexuality, which will destroy their reputation and their self-image. I prefer those with softer hands, and those without macho affectations. Because in addition to pain relief, part of what I look for in a massage is softness, tenderness and mothering. And men, whatever else they may be superb at, including algebra and genocide, are not their best at these.

On the other hand, as I care about and do passionately believe in equal rights for men—a most unfashionable but neglected subject—I know from a few online forums that whenever a male massage therapist writes a post saying that he is not getting enough business simply because he's male, he tends to get shouted down by colleagues who dislike the truth when it doesn't suit them or fit the politically correct platitudes of the moment. I do hope more and more men get well-paying jobs giving massages—not for just the men who prefer men, but jobs giving sensual massages to needy women starving for the touch of male hands. (As for myself I believe—or fantasize—I can do a pretty decent job of giving a woman a sensual massage, but I also suspect it is a lot harder work than it seems, being about 20 per cent inspiration and 80 per cent perspiration.)

INTERLUDE 1

THE GUANTANAMO-ING OF PENISES AND NIPPLES

It was in the spectacular island paradise of Samui, in the Gulf of Siam, around 2002, that all the psychological, social and legal borders that I had hitherto been aware of, between men and their masseuses, between men's bodies and masseuses' bodies, disappeared for me. Man and masseuse became one flesh, one loving bundle of throbbing, excited flesh. But until then, especially in America, the Berlin Wall between subject and masseuse often intrigued, troubled and vexed me. Or perhaps it was more like the Mexican American border, which at certain points of connection, like immigrant-hating Arizona for example, can be quite dangerous and even fatal to the 'intruder'.

True, thanks to training and licensing requirements for massage therapists in many Western countries, sometimes requiring two years of study, there is far more professionalism and far fewer untrained amateurs—except for holistic or new age types, who don't require licences in a few US states. In easy-going, laxly regulated countries like Thailand and Indonesia on the other hand, almost anyone can start working as a massage therapist, posing some risk of incompetent and medically risky massages.

But one drawback of some Western masseuses (and I include many countries mentally colonized by the West) is this feeling at the back of their minds: *Oh, I would love to massage the human body; if only half of them didn't come with penises attached.* They simply cannot accept the thought that the present model of man, created by an allegedly male God (conveniently created by male prophets), comes pre-fitted with that unholy thing called the penis, and they punish the poor man for it, making it (and him) shrink and cower and hide in its little dark corner. The manoeuvres they make to isolate, quarantine and neutralize the male snake are often so highly creative (and sometimes hilarious) that they merit five low whistles. Many a traditional American masseuse's attitude to a penis is like the traditional American response to terrorists: quarantine them in Guantanamo, where they can be isolated and prevented from attacking the American mainland.

But this artificial division between intimate parts and non-intimate parts is a division which our bodies simply don't recognize, which nature doesn't recognize, and which is, therefore, manmade and woman-made bullshit.

On the other hand, many an Oriental woman has no problem with the phenomenon of men having a fleshy appendage between their legs, whether hard or soft. Indeed, it's sometimes the opposite: because you have a penis, you are a blessed, sacred thing. Once, at a New York Korean massage spa near Penn Station, a Korean masseuse who on a previous occasion had given me a massage passed me in the men's locker room where I was towelling myself dry after a shower. And with a 'Hi' and an affectionate smile, she simply touched my penis lightly as she passed. (Lightly patted would also be correct, gently fondled would also describe it—'groped', certainly not.) That was it. It might have been a handshake, but since my penis was out and available and my hands busy towelling myself, it seemed more proper, even respectful, to greet my more essential and dominant part.

However, imagine if the reverse had happened: imagine if a male therapist had walked through the women's locker room and patted a woman affectionately on her vulva, the cops would have been there in five minutes, and the poor male therapist marched off to spend the next ten years of his life in a prison.

I also recall a masseuse I had called in to my hotel room in Songkhla, Thailand, and who had appeared anxious and nervous about me when she first entered my room (and I admit, I am not a sight for sore or terrorist-phobic eyes—except in the dark, when I am positively fearsome). Within twenty minutes, this mother of three grown daughters had become so comfortable and intimate with me that, while working on my upper back with her right hand, she rested her left hand on my right buttock for support, her fingers hovering around the entrance to my crack. This is one of the most comforting, trusting and touching gestures a human being can receive from another—a gesture which says: *Your body is like my body, I have ceased to feel any difference or separation of identities between us, and I can use parts of you for support without asking for your permission.* It is a beautiful and intimate and warm gesture. Absolutely no fear and trembling about New York state law or lawsuits alleging violation or sexual harassment.

Far more intimate were my massages with Yu, twenty-seven, another Thai masseuse, who in the beautiful little Gulf of Thailand island of Koh Samui became my girlfriend for a while, a part-time girlfriend rather, because, though our intimacy had spilled over into strong sexual attraction, treading on to the realm of love (or so I felt), I would still pay her for the massage (plus a good tip) and she would return to her massage joint, though later she took a week off to live with me in Bangkok. While she was massaging my arm or chest, say, one of my hands would cup her tits, or I would insert a finger inside her pussy and leave it there; nothing like resting your finger in the best and warmest possible spot, the sacred spot. Why not rest one's hand or finger on the bed, you ask? Because that's boring, one is doing it every day. Life is short. You don't have a loving woman in intimate surroundings every day, and this is a gift one can never take for granted—as months and months of post-divorce existence in the New York desert taught me.

The other cool thing about Thai masseuses: Anatomy may be sacred and God-given, and indeed it is, but it is also comical at times. So if a Thai masseuse finds your pecker standing up or staying resolutely sideways over your thigh and thus obstructing the course of the sacred Thai massage, she will laugh—sometimes laughing really hard at a dick that seems to be pointing at her or following her around like a pet one-eyed puppy, which this amazing creature can sometimes end up impersonating. And perhaps a masseuse might tickle or touch it playfully, or make a joking comment. Even if this playful conversation or touching is the limit of how far she intends to go, there's no reason to be a prim stuck-up ass and not laugh along with her. For the nice thing about her laugh (including the laugh of Veronica, my Catholic catskills masseuse, who was pretty earthy, used the word 'stiffy' for erection, and had a low tolerance for bullshit), especially if you laugh along with her, is that it relaxes you—you can see the humour of it, rather than feel guilty and have to try to explain your erection. This is something that my high-strung long-time New York masseuse Janet lacked. Though 95 per cent of the time I was being massaged by her, and when I was lying nude face up, I had an erection pointing at the ceiling, she never acknowledged it . . . and I was always kept guessing. Should I have felt embarrassed, proud, indifferent, or hypocritically joined in her pretence that it didn't exist?

Indeed, this particular Thai masseuse, massaging my inner thigh from behind, finds her finger obstructed by my glans or penile knob, and yet she repeats her move, twice or thrice. She's not going to let a wayward and truant penis obstruct her in her professional duties as a loyal Thai masseuse, is she? And hurray to that! Hurray to the professional dedication of the Thais!

But, to return to the philosophical issue of what is body and what is not-body: There are those masseuses who in their attempts to avoid, at all costs, contamination by the Big P (pecker, penis, peepee—your choice), arm themselves in a manner calculated to elicit respectful whistles from the designers of the Reaganut's Star Wars space shield; their attempts are so heroic they recall the Dutch boy who, to prevent a dyke from flooding his country, plugged a hole with his finger (or his pecker, according to certain subversive alternative historians). But such efforts are doomed, as demonstrated by the philosophical exploration that follows, and which is a tiny bit more sophisticated than 'Hey, the love muscle is also a *muscle*, right?! So isn't it your job to release my *muscular* tension?'

Consider: once you begin to break down matter, you first get molecules, then atoms, and then protons, electrons, neutrons, bosons, and so on and on (and perhaps even a few morons), and plenty of empty space in-between. And so, despite any optical illusions to the contrary, despite any illusions of separateness, the body is nothing but one big, gaping hole or circus tent in which neutrons, protons and electrons are whizzing about like berserk fleas high on amphetamines, head atoms are shooting the breeze with foot atoms, penis atoms are exchanging telephone numbers and friendly hugs with non-penis atoms, and butt atoms are doing it to groin atoms from behind. The borderline between the one and the other, between arms and abdomen, between shoulders and peckers, is merely imaginary, a thing of infinite chaos and blindness, which not even the most advanced microscopes can detect.

It would help, therefore, for the sake of everyone's sanity and the sanity of the planet, to think of the entire male body as nothing but the extension of a penis, whose humble and sometimes cunningly disguised slave it is. So the male body is, if you wish, a sub-penis, a proto-penis, a friend and slave of the penis. Therefore, your attempt to fool yourself that you are preserving intact your heavenly virtue and your anti-penile hymen by not crossing the line between penis and not-penis is only a matter of degree, a self-engendered delusion. A delusion similar to a few fanatic Hindu vegetarians' insistence that *no* one who has *ever* touched meat be allowed to eat in their kitchens or off their plates. Yes, I know one such person, an Indian Marwari businessman, who lives in a dog-eating East Asian country and potters around town in a mini-van built by beef-eating Americans, employing a superbly efficient local secretary who is not allowed to enter his kitchen because she is a meat-eater. But what if the vegetable seller who sold him the vegetables helped himself to a beef kebab while on his snack break, and then, without washing his hands, touched the vegetable that he ended up eating? Similarly, what if the massage customer's hands had touched his sacred personal lingam when having a pee, thus polluting his hand with sacred lingam flakes, molecules, atoms or subatomic particles? Shouldn't the masseuse, to avoid contamination, also avoid touching her male customers' *hands*?

In conclusion, it seems rather arbitrary and fascist to me to so violate the human rights of a particular patch of skin when, after all, we may be nothing more than a congregation of atoms with an inflated sense of self-worth.

And now for a word from and on behalf of our nipples (clarification: as I have not interviewed enough women to elicit *their* opinions on nipples, the words that follow are spoken only on behalf of the neglected and mute nipples of *man*kind): Why are nipples, and sometimes the one-inch area surrounding them, left meticulously untouched by many Western or Western-influenced masseuses, who steer clear of them the way American convoys in Iraq and Afghanistan regard improvised explosive devices?

I imagine the thinking behind it is this: '*But your nipples are erogenous, so they ought not to be massaged. Or else, I would be giving you an erotic massage—which I, being a pure moral being and direct descendant of the Virgin Mary, sure as hell will not*.' My counter-question is: At what point precisely does sexual excitement begin? How many giddy and tumescent neurons make the quorum that tip a male over into the realm of sexual excitement? I remember the masseuse who, while massaging my chest, gave 7–10 broad strokes skirting around and isolating my nipples (which her massage school had probably warned her was red alert area), and in doing so made me feel weirdly uncomfortable, as if she had arbitrarily divided my skin into two warring zones, untouchable North Korea and friendly South. For in the process, she made my nipples feel touch-hungry, touch-mad, rejected, discriminated against, and deprived of its human and nipple rights (even though the most honourable Al Gore did not lose control, despite his masseuse's allegations, my nipples, if they had hands, could easily have lost control with such a masseuse, especially if she had nipple-starved them after months of having been so generously treated by Asian masseuses). In any case, how could this masseuse be sure that massaging my neck didn't excite me sexually? Or the back of my knee? Every spot in my body is potentially erotic, and every soft touch is potentially erotic as well, the particularities varying from person to person. So the only way to frustrate or completely squash any sexual excitement is either to use sandpaper gloves (and be prepared for a lawsuit or worse), or abandon the massage profession altogether and enter a cloistered convent. Besides which, what a hateful, ungenerous, perverted attitude to life—to so micromanage it as to scrupulously *avoid* giving pleasure!

Besides, if you massage a person and he sweats, are you giving him a sweat massage? If he feels ticklish, is it because you are giving a tickling massage? Or if you massage someone's thigh, and he has an erection, or even an ejaculation, how grandiose of you to imagine that you are giving him a sex massage! If a woman were to have an orgasm because I gave her a back rub, even a free back rub, I would exclaim, 'Hallelujah! More power to her and her sexuality! She's definitely going to go through her life happy happy happy!' Because, what does it have to do with me? It's her lucky and blessed body, not mine! Get rid of this omnipotent fallacy that you and you alone are the cause of everything.

A touch of the hands can be erotic; even a conversation, the tone of the voice, say while uttering such innocent words as 'Is the pressure right for you?' can be erotic. That is part of the mystery and fascination of the human mind, our inability to predict and remote-control human responses, including our own. Some women can arouse me by massaging my palms and my forearms, not usually erogenous zones for 95 per cent of the human race—I mean, truly, such a woman's touch could sometimes pump vast quantities of blood into the spongy tissue between my legs. And yet, I guarantee even a Ku Klux Klan jury would burst into tears and feel compelled to award me massive damages for a massage in which my forearms were starved of touch.

At other times, the flanks of my upper body are erotic. My nipples are most often aroused, yet there is nothing more frustrating and killing in a massage than the feeling that the masseuse's hands have skirted the nipples, leaving a large area of epidermis around it untouched and starved! 'Discrimination!' my nipples scream, and launch into a brief adaptation of Shylock's speech in *The Merchant of Venice*: 'Why leave *us* out? What harm have we done to you? Is it our fault that we are nipples and not toes? Don't we also need touch, warmth, love?'

Eroticism and sex are all in the mind. Sometimes, a female hairdresser giving me a haircut with love, affection and lack of self-consciousness can make me feel sexy and aroused. I have had an erection while being treated by one of my best dentists ever—a woman doctor at the Bangkok Christian hospital. Were they giving me sex? Should they therefore stop cutting my hair or treating me? At other times, I have had real intercourse that was so mechanical and depressingly devoid of tenderness or passion that I would have preferred a haircut from the right woman instead.

The lesson: Sex is in the head. To try to control one's sexual response is to try to control one's mind. Do not try, because you cannot.

PART III

ORIENTAL MASSAGE: SOUTHEAST ASIA AND CHINA

Not only are massage establishments in Malaysia and Singapore often staffed by masseuses from Thailand, Indonesia, the Philippines and China, but there are some similarities in the massage landscape across the Southeast Asian region, especially in the attitudes of these cultures—a tolerant, easy-going, non-judgemental, erotically positive approach, with a belief in live and let live, plenty of warm smiles (though not in China), and above all, an uncomplicated love of laughter, pleasure and happiness.

Some Indian readers may be as surprised as I was to learn that the Thai massage was founded by Jivaka Komarabhacca (or Shivago Komarpaj in Thai legend)—an Indian. He was a contemporary of the Buddha, and was his personal physician and a physician to hundreds of his monks. While this fact would naturally be a source of pride to Indians, as it is to me, it is also reasonable to assume that the modern Thai massage is a blend of Chinese and other Southeast Asian influences and healing traditions.

7

FOOL BAWDY MASSAGE

In any one of the dozen cities and pleasure zones of Pleasurelandia, which is a region more than a country, you have to just walk down the street, practically any street of any town or city, sometimes just walk outside your hotel or stroll on the beach, and sooner rather than later, you will find yourself engaged in variations of the following conversation:

Want massage, sir?

No.

Bawdy massage.

No!

Hole bawdy massage.

No!!!

Good for you, sir. Make happy.

No. (Hey, life is short. No point wasting your exclamation marks.)

Fool bawdy massage, sir. *Fool* bawdy.

Massage *everything*? (At this point, curiosity, resignation, amusement and playfulness have overtaken, melted or atomized your initial feelings of suspicion, cynicism and irritation.)

Yes, *everything,* sir!

Including what? (You want to be really sure there's no catch. Besides, you're the sort who likes to know the score.)

Include *fool* bawdy. But not include ping pong.

How about *pong*?

Ok, *pong*, he responds—pong being the Cambodian word for egg.

Two pongs, ok?

Ok, two pongs. But *ping* pong extra.

Not interested. I was just joking, my friend! Ha ha! You want to make my ping pong go ding dong, eh?!

Ha ha ha, sir.

Ha ha ha to you, my friend.

(After a pause, he recovers his poise and coolly asks:) You want *bawdy to bawdy* massage, sir?

Really?

Bawdy to *bawdy*, sir.

Really? Wow!

Yes, sir. Lady take off everything. Nakkid nakkid, sir. And massage you with *hole* bawdy. *On your hole bawdy.*

Really?

Velly velly good, sir.

And ping pong?

Ping pong massage, sir, afterwards.

Include?

Not include, sir. Extra. Fool bawdy include massage with mew. With milk. But not take out your water.

My water?

Yes, your ping pong water.

That is extra?

Yes, sir.

Ok, how much for everything, dammit?

1,000 baht, sir. Make happy happy, sir. Make ping pong happy, sir. Sleep velly good. Yes, velly good!

Happy happy, eh? How about happy happy happy? Would that be 500 baht more than just happy happy?

Yes, sir. Too happy. Happy maak maak.

Include boom boom?

No, sir. Boom boom 1,000 baht extra.

Why extra? (Of course you know why. You're just being perverse, having fun with the questions.)

You want *massage boom boom*? With beautiful lady, sir. Have *movie star*.

Hmmm, movie star. Let me guess. Is her first name Angelina, by any chance?

No, sir. Angel.

Oh. And has this Angel starred in any movies that I may have seen?

Don't know, sir. Maybe . . . if you have seen *Thai Angels XXX No. 23*.

(*Thai Angels*! Movie star! Even a hardened man's resistance has begun to melt.) How much?

1,000 baht for beautiful lady. 2,000 baht for sexy lady. 3,000 baht for karaoke singer. 4,000 baht for movie star. In loom 1,000 extra.

You mean in *room* 1,000 extra.

Yes, sir. In loom 1,000 extra. But no bawdy to bawdy.

Why?

Because bawdy to bawdy lady not same lady as massage boom boom lady. Also extra for karaoke.

Karaoke? What made you think, all of a sudden, that I was looking for a musical evening?

Karaoke, sir. Lady smoke your banana, sir! Make *kala-okay* with your banana, sir. Velly good. Velly healthy, sir. Sleep velly good.

Oh, I see. And I thank you from the bottom of my heart for being so concerned about my sleep, my health and my general welfare. But let me get this straight: smoking-hot lady sing karaoke with and smoke my banana, but no light it on fire, right?

Ha ha, yes sir. No worry, sir, she no barbecue your banana, sir, no light your fucking ass on fire . . . sir!

So karaoke include? (By now, you understand that 'karaoke' is their comical slang for fellatio, and you have also picked up a bit of the local 'English', or Thinglish, Minglish or Singlish, in which there are no tenses except the present.)

Ha ha, sir. No, sir. 500 *extra* for karaoke.

Ok, forget all that. I was just joking. How much for a simple massage? Massage *no* boom boom.

Solly, sir. Massage *no* boom boom *no* have. You want massage no boom boom, you go beauty salon. Closed now, open tomollow molning.

At this point you are likely to be so frustrated that you throw your hands in the air and say, 'Okay, just give me everything. And take *all* my money! And take me too! My cherry is still intact.'

Because at this moment, your wheels or your chakras are spinning, and that is the worst moment for someone to switch off the power. Because while you may have thought *you* were playing him, the fact is that *he* was playing *you* all along. He has come across a hundred wise guys like you, and there is a 50–50 chance that you will at this point crumble and take whatever is on offer. Because he has subtly sold himself, even if you thought at first you were going to have some fun at the poor local joker's expense. Your mojo wheels that are spinning must now either be taken care of, or you won't be able to sleep—or worse, may have to check into the local nuthouse, and you can't let yourself down like that. It's like being in a swank and cavernous but windowless New Delhi restaurant on a summer afternoon when suddenly there is a power failure, and the air-conditioner stops and the lights go off.

Many of us will have surrendered at some half-way point in the above dialogue, if not earlier, and be stretched out on a massage table or on a bed, having the wildest time of our lives, sensuality spiced with laughter and total insanity, a scenario we couldn't even have begun to dream of in our own countries. Because once our arousal has proceeded beyond the point of containment by logic, we are like lambs led to the slaughter. Helpless and pitiful. At this point, only the physical intervention of Superman can save our souls.

Besides, some of us are here precisely because of this insatiable desire for touch, for laughter, closeness and intimacy (whether or not we admit it to ourselves), of which the world, including parts of the Western and Eastern worlds, has not enough.

8

UNTRADITIONAL THAI MASSAGES

Nothing about twenty years of living in America, and a bit more than that of living in India before that, had prepared me for what I was to discover in Thailand. At first, I would just stop over there for 3–4 days on my New York to India trips, planning to break my jet lag and help myself to a few of its world-famous cheap massages, and thus prepare for the hard work and sexless weeks I expected in India. But after a bad divorce in which I lost custody of my children, in a difficult period from 1999 through mid-2000, and partly because of Southeast Asia's comparatively low cost of living, a dollar or two for a meal, as little as fifteen dollars a night for an air-conditioned room, and seven dollars for a massage—my objective now having changed to survival, emotional, physical and financial, until I published a commercially successful book—I started spending long stretches in Thailand and Indonesia, month after month, always planning for a month or two each time. Unexpectedly, all of these months added up to over three years spent in Thailand and Indonesia combined, and two more years in other Southeast Asian countries. And on these trips, I took my willy along with me, which, according to one wise guy on the Internet, is one of just two things a man gets to keep after a divorce (frankly, I still don't know what the other one is).

'What was all the stress about? Aren't you going to tell us about the catastrophe in your life?' said Pam, my blonde editor, who had provided the deep editing for my novel, as well as the comforting that every writer needs when he is working on difficult, emotional material. We were spread out naked on the rug in her Upper West Side apartment.

'Please, I can't tell them about it here,' said I. 'I need a completely different book, a new one, to do it justice—anything less would be superficial.'

'Fine then, I'll have to take your word for it,' she said, looking disappointed. Then brightening, she added, 'Well then, isn't it time to tell them about the breasts?'

'Okay, then. Briefly, I found myself in a scenario I couldn't have imagined in my wildest dreams: totally cut off from my children, spouse, home and society. For someone who had lived for years with much affection from my family, it now assumed a greater importance than ever before—not just intimacy with a woman, but mouth-to-mouth kissing. I tongue-kissed anyone who would let me kiss them, sometimes perfect strangers—so long as they unambiguously belonged to the female sex, which can be an illusory distinction in Thailand with its gorgeous and often convincing lady boys, I admit. No doubt it would often lead to sex, but guess what? Western psychiatrists don't tell you this—because they want repeat business from you, and do not want you to be cured. But I have conclusively discovered that, for a man, the most effective antidepressant is a loving woman's arms, and her soulful mouth-to-mouth kisses, followed by or interwoven with sex.

'At first, after a month's visit to Thailand, when my Thai tourist visa expired, I would return to the US. Back there I would find myself isolated and in an emotional wasteland, for there was only so much fun and comfort that one could get from mocking one's own sadness by singing along with Ray Charles's blues. So I began to plot spending more of my time in Southeast Asia, overcoming visa time limits by moving from country to country, and

sometimes crossing the border for just a few days, or for fifteen minutes, and returning to Thailand.

'Then I discovered that massage need not be merely massage, but a quick way to intimacy . . . sometimes, nay often, the masseuse herself being someone who had been jilted in love, or abandoned by a lover or a spouse after being impregnated or left holding the baby, and who, like me, was seeking tenderness and affection. And when I sensed that, we were instantly attracted to each other, overflowing with healing love.

'This is the unspoken element in all of this narrative, post-2000—the explosive, almost insatiable desire to be intimate with a woman, have my skin brush against hers, and suck on a lovely breast, whenever I could—some of the most beautiful and tender of the massages that occurred after 2000 would be those in which a woman, usually Southeast Asian, would offer me her breast to suck, yes, right in the middle of the massage. Where in the entire boring New York State massage law is there a provision for such a thing, and where in the next million years will there ever be one (dream on, you patriots and cheerleaders for the American way)? I wanted to run as far away from New York as I could; I wanted to be in a land where kindness and tenderness were not measured or doled out in coffee spoons, prices regulated naturally by New York State sales or service tax . . .'

'There, there,' said Pam. 'Don't get so emotional. Suck on mine. After all, my nipples are pink. Your favourite colour.' I obliged.

'Hey, don't stop. I'm not finished with you yet,' said Pam. 'You better clarify this question for your socially sensitive readers: All these masseuses, perhaps 700 different ones all over the world—how did you know they were not your slaves?'

'How do they know you're *not one, that you're not someone I keep chained in a basement?' I said. She laughed, and waited.*

'Okay then,' I said. 'Let me make this clear: my masseuses in the US, that is, the ones I patronized 95 per cent of the time, were overwhelmingly white women, and mostly independent. None of them walked around with chains attached to their legs. Well, though a few of them may have been mental

slaves of Gaia, the new age goddess, or of television, or of the "system", physical slaves they were not, for they usually drove home, at the end of the day, to their families or boyfriends—unless, as in many cases, they were operating from their own homes or apartments.

'Then, from 2000 to 2009, when I received most of my massages in Asia, they were still overwhelmingly pure massages. But sometimes, they would end in sex. Which usually happened in the aftermath of my traumatic personal experience from early 1999 to 2003, and very rarely in recent years, when my massages have once again become strictly massage. Such an occurrence would usually be the unplanned result of some combination of chemistry, personal initiative and excess libido, outside the massage parlour, either in my hotel room if she had paid a house call, or during a date outside the parlour and without the permission or knowledge of her employers. Sometimes, it was I who was seduced, and many or nearly all of these women told me later that they usually had sex just once or twice a month, and in rare cases once or twice a week, and were often sex-starved for months, because the local men saw them as "over the hill"—divorced or single mothers. And in every case in which we made love, and a few times when we didn't, I would suck on their breasts, and four out of five times, they would be so affected as to draw my head closer and close their eyes while I was doing it. Which I found very moving.

'And that was when I think I understood something about those twin points of feminine attraction that so moved men, and how traumatic it must have been for them to be separated from their mothers' breasts when they were infants. My guess is that a girl, who will sooner or later develop her own breasts, which are an integral part of her, does not feel this trauma of separation as much, if at all. She knows she'll soon have breasts herself, and will be in a position to share what she has. This explains the magnetic attraction that men have towards breasts, which are often the first feminine feature to catch a man's attention—unless he is behind her, in which case it is her globular buttocks, with their breast-like cleavage, to which his eyes almost unconsciously gravitate. Are there men for whom this does not happen?

Perhaps, but that may be because they have been "corrected" and "educated" by the requirements of "polite society" into believing that it is improper to look at a woman's breasts.

'And why did the women respond thus to me? My guess is that the mothering instinct is never completely extinguished in a woman, no matter how modern, liberated, single or childless she may be. Thus it is that a kitten, or a baby animal, or a human baby, nearly always excites a woman far more than it excites the average man: she wants to hold it, pet it, snuggle it close to her chest—or her breast. And that was when I understood the appeal of my Indian friend and co-visitor to Thailand, outside whose door every morning I would notice a dainty pair of women's shoes, the Thai equivalent of a "Do Not Disturb" door sign. He told me that his secret was to spend 15–30 minutes exclusively pleasuring women's breasts, to approach them from fifteen different directions with a different move each time. They had never experienced anything like it before. Once he did that, they were all his for the taking.'

But all this happened later. When I first visited Thailand, landing up in the city of life and brazen pleasure, Bangkok, with its signs such as 'Darling Turkish Bath,' 'Pussy Show' and 'Sexy Teen Massage', and women visible everywhere—vibrant, standing tall, aggressive, and often running the city, the shops, everything but the buses and taxis and police stations—I was bowled over by how easy and relaxed the Thai masseuses were with the human body, with the body of the complete stranger they were massaging, and what a peaceful and even playful thing a massage in their hands could be. As with this masseuse, Nu, a mother in her thirties. Once I flop face-down and naked onto my rubber-sheeted foam mattress for my oil massage, she draws the blue screen partition around me to shield my nakedness from peeking eyes, and then treats my body as if it were her two-year-old baby's. Her strokes have the fluidity and grace of a champion rowing a boat, the forward and return movements so easily blending into one continuous rolling motion. For part of this massage she is sitting beside your buttocks, drawing her hands up your inner thighs, and gently giving a feather-soft massage to your gratefully expanding balls before circling around your buttocks and reaching down towards your knees. It is almost as if she had been born to do this. You don't discern the slightest conflict in her as you would in the masseuses of certain other countries, who must ceaselessly battle with an internal tormentor and puritan censor who harangues them with the suggestion that what they are doing is not respectable, or that certain parts of the body are 'dirtier' than others.

And their names! Even listening to the names of the Thai masseuses is enough to make me laugh out loud and relax me. For only in Thailand could you be massaged by a Pook (the sound of a fart), who may have earned her name by farting at the moment of birth. I have also been massaged by Fon (rain), besides Meow (cat), Nok (bird), Mot (ant), Goong (shrimp), Yo, Poom, Boom and Pooh (crab).

After the first time I entered Thailand, this knowledge of the complete acceptance of my body, this promise of warmth and uncomplicated sexuality, had made such an impression on me that the moment I landed in Bangkok on subsequent occasions and stepped into the taxi to get to my hotel, an indescribable calm and joy would slowly sink into me, making me feel generous towards humankind—optimistic and grateful. And I would think, 'What a gracious people. How lucky I am to be here.'

Why Standing Up?

In many a Thai or Southeast Asian massage parlour, any statement such as 'Thai massage' or 'body massage' is simply an opening statement—there are no defined categories, and anything can turn into something else, all depending on the situation and the mood. Words and their limited connotations don't prevent the Thais from being human and extremely flexible. Especially if something is 'standing up'.

As with Meow. Meow, long dark hair, beautiful eyes, is called in to my beachside hotel room in the Kamala Beach section of Phuket, an island in the sun surrounded by blue waters and a blue sky adorned by a few powder puff clouds. The hotel's lavish rooms are located in independent bungalows set on a terraced hillside, each bungalow with its own view of the sea, framed by gardens and trees. Minutes after I call the receptionist and order an oil massage, Meow arrives at my door with a basket full of scented oils and creams and small towels, smiling, wai-ing, or offering me the traditional Thai folded-hand greeting, her body language signalling an absolute eagerness to please. She's wearing white shorts and so is her companion, a trainee, an unexpected gift who will also massage me as part of her learning process. In hotel rooms, the Thai masseuses, who are usually short, climb on to the usually king-sized bed and, in a sense, climb over you from various directions, thus becoming an adjunct to your body. Sometimes they sit on top of your bum or thighs, and sometimes they stand on your body. Admittedly, when they stand on your body, you better protect your balls, or at least pray for them, but the rest of the massage is relaxed and intimate. You rarely encounter the strict separation of roles that you find in Western massages, in which the masseuse is the director, the boss, the doer; whereas you, the customer, are the passive recipient, and better not make any sudden moves unless you are eager to face molestation charges.

The comely Meow massaged me nude (I was nude, she fully clothed), often nonchalantly brushing over my penis, or letting it nuzzle against her elbows or forearms, warming them and passing on some electrical energy while she massaged my belly. In other words, the penis to her was not an object of dread, but simply another democratic member of the physical world, like a lamp, or a tree, or a rock, or a pencil, except that this was a thicker pencil covered with skin and topped by a brown-pink hat. There was no need to inconvenience herself or me simply because of a piece of elongated flesh, an object of variable length, no need to get a crick in her neck or a strained muscle because of having to bend or perform a gymnastic manoeuvre just to avoid touching the evil snake. And as her hands roamed freely over my belly, her forearms kept brushing nonchalantly against a now completely vertical cock, resulting in a sudden spray of sticky white fluid into the ecosphere. An embarrassing moment for me, yet she, without a flap, without a heart attack, and without a word, simply picked up a towel from the chair, wiped clean the evidence, and then, with Buddha-like aplomb, continued with her massage. I could have embraced her for that acceptance, for that naturalness, for not putting me on the spot or grilling me like a grand inquisitor for that innocent biological accident. Only way towards the end, about half an hour later, when her proximity to my pecker provoked a second erection did she ask me if I wanted her to 'take care' of it (quite a few Thai women that I have met seem to have this endearing motherly concern about 'taking care' of you). Until then, nothing in her demeanour had suggested that she would even honour such an obscene request had it come from me.

Meow, being a little older (perhaps twenty-seven), was a bit sedate, lacking the playful humour I found in Pooh, the nineteen-year-old girl with a baby-doll haircut who had given me an untraditional (me nude, masseuse in sexy white shorts) Thai massage the previous day, and who was so natural, so much at peace with life, that she just pushed my penis away when it obstructed her lawful path, sometimes watched it in wry amusement, and at other times mock-seriously scolded it as she might a naughty two-year-old boy, '*Why standing up?! Why not go to sleep?!*' Why indeed? An eternal question, standing tall in comparison with 'To be, or not to be?' or, 'What is the meaning of life?'—Pooh's question, even more than the other two, is a question that I have pondered on for decades without much enlightenment. At other times, Pooh would playfully shake her finger at my erect dick and then take matters into her own hands: she would push the insensible and recalcitrant thing down to 'sleeping' position to make her point. And she was so relaxed as she climbed over me and crossed over me, my big feet and long fingers at times touching, or brushing against, her breasts and her pussy; she was so absorbed in the Zen of giving me a massage, as if her comfort, and my comfort, and the massage itself, were all that mattered, that two separate identities had merged, at least for the time being. She was no more going to twist her body into unnatural shapes for 'modesty's sake' than a cat would, for modesty's sake, lift up its behind and tilt its body so that its balls wouldn't touch and thus possibly contaminate its owner's sofa.

The Hotel Call-In Massage

This is the kind of massage where you respond to one of the phone numbers in the maps, tourist brochures or 'guides' which are full of advertisements whose main interest is to provoke your lust and relieve you of your cash. Many of these numbers offer round-the-clock service, unlike the hotel's own massage staff, if any.

One worker I spoke to, Nan, said that she was once called in by a white couple who wanted two female masseuses to massage them simultaneously; the two masseuses were then asked to touch their private parts, and then were made to watch the couple make love. She had a big and unattractive pussy, and his cock was small. Nan and her friend were embarrassed. She and her partner have also refused requests for enacting lesbian shows for customers' voyeuristic pleasure, though she's open to a threesome or foursome, especially a threesome, because in a threesome with two girls, it is half the work and double the pay—for one of the two girls usually gets off lightly.

No Undie Sit on You Massage

Another widely prevalent Thai technique or trick (depending on your perspective), or massage style, is the 'No Undie Sit on You' massage. The trick, especially used when they are massaging you in your room on the bed, or on a mat or mattress on the floor, is for the masseuse to sit on top of your buttocks while she massages your back. Since most Thai masseuses are small and lightweight, unlike their foreign guests, this is not usually a problem, but an erotic provocation, because if they are lightly clothed, you can feel their warm pussies against your naked buttocks, and this can be very sexy indeed, especially since sometimes, from the pressure, you can sense whether they have pubic hair or none (a mental exercise that can do wonders for your right brain, by the way, and should be a prescribed routine for courses in creative thinking).

The first time it happened, the masseuse, Goong, sent to me by an outcall service, had come in wearing a thin jogging suit of sorts, and when she sat on my nude buttocks, her pussy—yes, her pussy and its surrounding area—rubbed against my bare posterior through pretty thin clothing, and such exquisite pleasure it gave my id-ruled brain that the wicked idea came to my mind that in future a legislation should be passed that all massages ought to be performed without panties. As if this weren't maddeningly erotic enough, the tops of her soft, tender, amazingly flexible feet lay inverted on the backs of my upper thighs and buttocks, with the toes sneakily curving up towards my pelvic fulcrum—any moment now, I thought, a toe of hers could, like some heat-seeking Phantom missile, seek out and tickle my cock and perhaps, as a result, find itself receiving a creamy shower of love.

The other common Southeast Asian massage technique is where the masseuse sits astride you, or her pelvis floats a couple of inches above you, with her knees on the bed or on the massage table, while she massages your back. When she bends to reach your upper back during her upward movement, her pubis or pussy makes contact with your buttocks: thlap, shlap! As this movement is a circular, repeated movement, again and again, the pussy returns to say hello to your buttocks, and if you have any life left in you at all, your erotic arousal is going to be pretty close to exploding point.

A few years later, in a small Southeast Asian town in which most of the commercial establishments were housed in shacks, and there was only one Internet cafe that worked only one-third of the time, I was desperate for a massage, and agreed to be massaged by the only masseuse available at that moment: a Vietnamese woman of around sixty, who sat on me in her traditional Vietnamese tight silk pajamas, with no undies underneath. Soon, by purposefully rubbing her thinly veiled vulva against my middle one-third while pretending to be innocent and to be concentrating on the purely therapeutic, she caused a massive and hugely embarrassing erection, which reminded me that sex is all in the mind: the mere thought of the woman's undie-less state and her erotic intention was the trigger, and it didn't matter one bit that she was sixty years old!

But the 'no undie' theme is distracting me from my subject: Thailand, and the contrast between the liberated and relaxed countries of East Asia, and puritanical America, where I had resided for a good part of my adult and massage-receiving life.

Liberating the Puritan sections of the West

From the noble, virtuous, sincere, highly professional and scrupulously law-abiding massage therapists of my American, German and, occasionally, British experience to the brown sex apsaras of Southeast Asia disguising themselves as masseuses—what a journey! For in my years of ignorant, naïve and wasted youth in India (the waste carrying on, unforgivably, for twenty years beyond my youth, well into my middle age), salivatingly watching Hollywood movies with their Marilyn Monroes and Raquel Welches, I had believed that sexual liberation could *only* be found in the *West*. After all, the West had produced Henry Miller and had invented orgies and free love (or so I thought), so it would be the duty of the West to spread this liberation and enlightenment to the rest of the world—the *new* white man's and white woman's burden, right?

How mistaken I was! It is Thai, Chinese, Korean and Japanese masseuses (and some masseurs) who, emigrating in droves in the last few decades to Paris, London, New York, Toronto and Los Angeles, have with missionary zeal set in motion the process that the Bush-whacked world really needs: the liberation and loosening of the once-uptight regions of the West, and of countries such as India and Dubai. In 2009, I discovered happy ending shops disguised as massage joints in nearly every third block in parts of Manhattan, approximately one for every five sushi joints (though I have no idea about the precise relationship between the two—they seem to have expanded more or less in tandem)!

Though uninterested in hand jobs, I am a last-minute emergency massage seeker who can't deal with cold and inhuman messages from answering machines, or a 3–5 day waiting period for appointments preceded by a screening interview—all of which are usual with American-born therapists. In contrast, recent immigrant Chinese and Korean joints often offer an immediate, reasonably competent, walk-in massage from someone who won't throw a whole puritan guilt trip on me for being a man and, therefore, a criminal until proven innocent.

As for the inevitable offer of a hand-job, what can you do? If you're for it, go ahead, and don't count on me to give you a lecture on morality. But if not, just say *no*.

9

THE THAI SANDWICH MASSAGE

It should be a universal right enshrined in the UN Human Rights Charter: that every human being is entitled to receive at least one sandwich massage during his or her lifetime.

It was in the back streets of hot, humid and wild Pattaya, a former fishing village turned into a pleasure resort for American G.I.s on a rest-and-recuperation break from Vietnam, and now the sin-sun-and-sea capital of Thailand, that this story takes place. It was here, in one of those massive temples of massage, with parking lots as large as football fields, that I discovered the concept of a sandwich massage. At first it was just an item on a menu, an item whispered to me by some Lucifer-inspired tout on a Pattaya street ('Sir, sandwich massage, sir?'), but when I began to understand what was being proposed, I simply started laughing at the sheer lunacy of it, the sheer extravagant joyous life-affirming absurdity of it! In the age of AIDS! Begone, ye fellas! Get outta here, don't pull my leg! And how in God's name can you protect yourself against viral infections during a sandwich massage unless you are to encase yourself in a body suit—preferably an impenetrable space suit? And yet, stop and consider for a moment: what use is an AIDS-free life without a sandwich massage?

To rewind the story back to its very beginning: One evening some years ago, around the time my marriage was breaking up, I found myself in Pattaya, bored, having depressed myself by sitting in my room for two days with my laptop in front of me, writing. Afraid of AIDS, afraid of leaving my sheltered seaside hotel and venturing into the unknown. For a healthy male to be bored in Pattaya, the sin capital of Thailand, there must be something seriously wrong with him!

Well, actually, it did help that I had safely ensconced myself far away from the main pleasure zones in a fortress of a hotel called the Ambassador Hotel, located in Jomtien, an offshoot of Pattaya and around 6 km from downtown. The hotel fills you with a feeling of stupefaction and wonder: how do they build these massive structures, where do they get the balls to plan and finance them, and what in hell are these high-rises doing in some quiet corner of Thailand which, only fifteen years back, was a sleepy fishing village in which the only occupation for most men, when they were not fishing, was scratching their balls?

It is spacious, no doubt: high ceilings, large rooms, an expansive view of the sea and mountains and skyscrapers and beach, and of swimming pools so gigantic you could sail a yacht inside them, pools so huge I could see the waves forming in them from up there in my seventeenth-floor room. Coconut palms swayed on the beach, providing shade from the white-hot sun. The beach itself is a narrow washout, and may explain the relative emptiness and desolation of this concrete jungle, this insane construction by the greedy and egomaniac financiers who backed it.

The hotel boasts eight massive restaurants, each large enough to house and feed an army battalion; but the total number of souls eating in *all* of these restaurants on this Wednesday evening is . . . eight! I finally choose the Seafood Restaurant, and an army of waiters and hangers-on waits on . . . who? Me! Yes me, me and only me, who is no prince, no nobleman, no tycoon, but just a drifter, a rolling stone, an unknown writer! It's a megalomaniac's delight, this absurd turn of events in which an entire restaurant in a 4.5-star mega hotel is awaiting one man's pleasure. And you're not even some president of a republic or some big managing director, but a shiftless vagabond of the universe, without moorings, without a proper occupation or a proper income, without anything worthwhile to your name, yet you have the gall to order not a hamburger, not chicken fried rice, but . . . hold your breath, grilled plakapong nicoise. For the simple bloody reason that grilled plakapong nicoise at eighty baht sounds like something you haven't eaten, and is in fact the cheapest dish among the things you haven't eaten (you haven't eaten minced pigeon either, but that's about 300 baht, and you're a cheapo, you'll carry that poverty mindset in your head and into your grave, so banish the thought of minced pigeon in this lifetime). Besides which, the name 'grilled plakapong' has that indefinable ping—well, ping-pong—to it.

And how shall I describe what happened thereafter?

I went into town, see, determined to make up for two nights of senseless self-abnegation. I knew that to make up for the asinine sterility and emptiness of the previous two days, there would be a sandwich massage (hereinafter referred to as an SM™), and perhaps even more sinful pleasures later. So, a short taxi ride later, I walked into that Pleasure Room™, the Sabai room massage parlour.

Entering the gigantic building, which from the outside looked like a large theatre-cum-arts complex, I noticed something queer: lots of Chinese and Singaporean-looking males were sitting alone at tables seemingly sipping coffee or beer and gazing into the distance, as if at some vision, as if at God descending onto the Sabai room massage parlour while perched on top of a cloud. Then, as my eyes adjusted to the dim lighting, I realized that what they were looking at was a human fishbowl, or a glass partition behind which, under coloured lights, nearly a hundred girls were seated, arrayed in their resplendent, heavily made-up glory, and in pink or blue robes or Thai kimonos, with a plastic number pinned above their left breasts. Far more momentous than God descending on a cloud—a hundred Thai beauties seated on blue-velvet steps behind a glass partition, a few looking bored, but most looking directly at you, smiling, waiting to be chosen and taken.

I am such a rube, such an ancient prude in some things. Indeed, I feel shy and guilty about such things as choosing a woman solely on the basis of her beauty or figure, as if one were selecting a piece of meat without first having talked to it (which would be okay if it really was meat, or else your butcher might think you had gone bananas). Such cosmetically advantaged behaviour militates against everything I believe in, and yet, I didn't make the rules, and the glass partition and the language gap prevented communication, so the best I could do was not to choose based on the girl's beauty, but rather for some quality of soul, and not take too long doing it. After all, I hadn't dreamt of anything more than a sandwich massage, during which I now understood that one girl would be on top of me, and another under me, with me being the turkey in between—and somehow, a massage would be achieved. As I'm no huge aficionado of sandwiches, which I think of as the lazy man's food, it didn't make a lot of sense to me to worry about the composition of the sandwich when all I really wanted was a massage. Anyway, it wasn't a hard decision. It wasn't like I was trying to solve the Middle Eastern problem, it was just a massage of some type, for God's sake. So all I decided was to scout for someone with a smile, who seemed to be in a reasonably good mood, and whose eyes connected with mine. No. 107 had a cute face and shortish hair, and No. 141 had a deepish cleavage. Both seemed to be infused by an essential combination of sexiness, a peaceful aura and good humour. (But goodness knows I've not been a great judge of people before this, so let me not fart around as if I had made a great and wise decision—it was pure fluke!)

I chose them, we walked into the room, they stripped and wrapped themselves in towels. These fucking towels always throw me off—why can't people simply and naturally be naked and use the towels only when they need to dry themselves? To heck with all this modesty shit, we all know what our equipment looks like.

Anyway, they readied the water and the bubbles and, in a hilarious application of modern technology in this still-ancient-in-some-ways society, a plastic float of the kind that fat farts use to float on in swimming pools. And they gave me a towel to cover my modesty—which was a scream, because modesty I have none. I may have a host of other virtues—kindness, generosity, tenderness, intelligence, humour, piety, political acumen, geographical knowledge, soft sensuous hands, mathematical ability and trigonometrical acumen—but modesty, not an effing shred of it, thank God!

I don't know what their fucking problem was, but there were some silly remarks about India and Indians that I didn't get, except for one that seemed to be, 'You don't have a smell about you.' What?! I joked weakly in response, saying something about India being bigger than her and this room, too gigantic and diverse to make general statements about, without being ludicrous. And then nothing happened, and this slight malice and baggage of racial slights disappeared. One was a Laotian; the other I guessed was a Thai—which, with me being Indian–American, would make this an international sandwich, a wonderful manifestation and symbol of the new world order decreed by President George W. Bush.

And then the fun began!

We went into the water and got our uh-uhs wet, and they soaped me while I soaped them. They hadn't asked me for assistance in the soaping department, but as I believed in the proletarian brotherhood of labour, I tried hard to soap their difficult-to-reach (for them) nether regions, especially considering that under the cloak of this humanitarian and philanthropic labour that any NGO could be proud of, my fingers could feel their soft, spongy and hairless pussy lips . . .

Goodness gracious, the silky smoothness of those lips! What remarkable shaving expertise had produced those works of art! (I didn't realize, when I wrote this, that certain races, the Chinese for example, often produce women who naturally have little or no pubic hair, making shaving, and the environmentally unfriendly institution of disposable razors, unnecessary.) My admiration for them was high indeed, and like any connoisseur, I bent low to get a better vantage point from which to admire these wonders.

Meanwhile, the women were loosening up, and so were their thighs, their attitudes, their postures, and such admiration was now an eminently feasible thing. And then I lay down, as directed, on the plastic float, and that was when the merriment ascended into a heaven of invention and ecstasy. I was lying face down on the float, when suddenly I was drowned in the sensation of a soapy woman and her alabaster breasts applying themselves in circles on my back and buttocks, describing arcs of exquisite pleasure on them. Atomic particles of indeterminate size and shape comprising my skin, millions of individual nerve endings, joined in dancing and going berserk with surprise and ecstasy—such was the magic of the combination of soap, water, woman, nipples and wicked intent.

Suddenly, a pudendum—I mean a prime Thai hairless pussy—went smack smack smack into my balls (I was totally surprised at the resilience of those usually delicate and tender spheres), as the girl went wild with the joy of it. It was as if she was riding a roller coaster, but her major point of contact was her pelvic fulcrum, that meeting point of perineum, ass and pussy, which was sliding up and down my legs, thighs and buttocks, reminding me of the loony Texan B-52 commander in *Dr Strangelove or: How I Learned to Stop Worrying and Love the Bomb* who mounts a nuclear warhead and sails towards his target like a gleeful cowboy at a rodeo.

Now that I think about it, it was a damn good thing that I had some self-control, and that earlier that morning, the in-house hotel masseuse had milked me and drained me of excess sperm, for it would have been catastrophic, to say the least, had I ejaculated at this particular moment in the history of the Thai sandwich massage. My happy flag flew at full mast, proudly. It was a glorious day for my manhood, and a giant leap for Indiankind (or for a tiny moment of fantasy, so I think).

At some point in the proceedings, we arrived at the pure sandwich moment. This was when I had two swollen nipples, one slippery smooth mons, and two silky thighs under my nude body, and two nipples, one trembling vulva, and two smooth thighs on top of me, and the one on top was doing a fair bit of giddy rolling around.

How can I explain the glorious sensuousness of this? Think of a massage by two women, except that this one used not just the women's hands, but their breasts, bellies, thighs, buttocks and pussies—to give multiple and simultaneous massages at different points of contact, so that, if you were a polymorphously perverse individual (which I nearly am, except that I have zero erogenous feeling in my nails, hair and kneecaps), inclined to get orgasms from nearly every part of your body, you could theoretically be getting multiple orgasms coming in from every direction simultaneously, causing an orgasmic traffic jam to rival Mexico City at rush hour.

It surprises me now to think that I didn't faint with pleasure, as heroines sometimes do in the more explicit romantic novels as their blonde and blue-eyed heroes' rampant 'manhood' storms their tender, delicate and throbbing citadels or inner goddesses.

The sandwich was now accomplished. Was it over?

The girls now washed off the massive quantity of soap and bubbles from my body, I helping with the formalities, and somehow, as if we were following a script written in heaven, perhaps by some karmic St Peter, all three of us drifted towards the bed, where towelled 107 began massaging a partly towelled me.

Whereupon 141 joined us and loosened her towel, at which point I gently fondled her breasts, and she was cheerful enough about it. Now 107 also loosened up and casually held onto my sky-pointing missile—as if for support while spaceship earth was suddenly experiencing turbulence—while she discussed further plans for the evening. Needless to say, with such a weapon in her hand, she had an unassailable advantage over me in any such discussion. For she could easily drive her point home.

Which discussions, it turned out, were pretty thin on abstruse philosophical abstractions and pretty much to the point. Would I like to fuck the two of them she asked, quite plainly. As if I didn't believe in equal rights and the equality of all women, and would favour one over the other.

At first the price seemed an obstruction—1,000 baht each, on top of the 1,000 baht I had already paid at the desk for the sandwich, which I had apparently already consumed and digested by now, if not excreted—but then, my fabled male weakness came into play. Had I been Adam, I might have eaten the apple in line 2 of Genesis, no serpent or woman necessary, and the story would pretty much be over by line 3. For 107 still had my cock as a not unwilling prisoner in her hands and was making appreciative remarks about it to 141 (or so it seemed—my laughter had infected all of us and had elevated the general mood)—so what chance did I have of resistance?

So it was agreed on, and we did it, but what I remember most about this phase of the proceedings was those few seconds when I had two separate fingers in two separate cunts! Positive charges from one cunt flooded through my tremulously hungry and yearning fingers, across my electrified body and then passed back through another set of fingers into a second positive terminal, the second cunt, whereupon a doubled energy reflected back through me, to the first cunt. The sheer delightful and lunatic decadence of it!

Happy together! Suddenly, the syrupy old pop song had a meaning! How could it ever have meant just two people! Three is the natural number, the way it was meant to be! If three is a good enough number for the Holy Trinity, it sure is good enough for us unholy mortals.

These were generous girls—they kissed me, kissed and licked my body, licked and sucked my cock (I had to restrain them from overdoing this particular procedure, I had some vague and innocent idea that there was danger in it) and tongued my balls, caressed and fingered my back and bum . . .

These were happy broads!

No doubt the rich are happy, and happier than the poor, I thought (no, I didn't really think it then—I'm thinking it now, while writing this down back in my hotel room . . . so long as we're trying to be honest, let's be really honest, even if it's a silly fart of a truth such as this). Not because, as in Hemingway's famous retort to Scott Fitzgerald, the rich have more money, but because they can afford more sandwiches. More Norwegian salmon sandwiches. More club sandwiches. More caviar sandwiches. More international sandwiches. More *love sandwiches*. And because more women, unable to overcome the basic make-up of their natures, will naturally attempt to get into the pants of the rich and the famous. (Though what a burden it must be for these poor rich stiffs to keep their pants on and zipped.)

Returning to my two new Thai lovers: the women seemed to know, when we walked out of the massage area and into the lounge, that they had zoomed me up into a stratosphere of ecstasy and fulfilment. I was radiant. How could anyone not see it? It made me feel a smaller man not to acknowledge them as we approached the main hall, not to walk proudly with them hand in hand, but to slink away as if we had been occupying the same space by mere accident, my visit to this huge erotic massage emporium having been in the role of a plumber, accountant, or wall painter perhaps!

I was in the valley of death, dying a spiritual death for the past few years, a death decreed by fear. And thou, the AIDS-scourge of the world—*great sex,* which can throw ordinary caution and medical prudence to the winds—yes, great sex, which pooh-poohs the AIDS fear-mongers of mankind—has brought me out of it.

At the time I had my first sandwich massage, I wasn't liberated enough, and I still needed to *justify*, to myself, this departure from my normal limits of prudence and adventure. But I told myself: I am a writer. As would also have been the case had I been a gynaecologist, looking up women's skirts, fiddling with whatever is inside them, and taking care of their needs, it was all right for me to have a special massage.

We writers, we are peephole specialists. With bulging eyes. We bring you life raw-as-sushi sometimes, or with a little Tabasco sauce or masala added at other times, our own particular concoction, never quite what the doctor had advised.

And having experienced a sandwich massage, I have now come to the conclusion that it is, that it must be, a basic human right.

Will the world therefore please provide sandwich massages to its six billion residents? And why not, for God's sake? Surely, a UN agency can be created, and a Thai national appointed as Undersecretary for Sandwich Massage? Whereupon s/he can work for the universal right of every human being to life, liberty and one sandwich massage in every two years.

10

WILL SHE WILLY? HAPPY ENDINGS AND ECSTATIC ENDINGS

On one of my post-divorce visits to Thailand, I had left behind a blonde part-time girlfriend, Lucy, in New York. We had known each other rather briefly, but I had confessed to her my addiction to massages. A few days after my arrival in Thailand, Lucy sent me an anxious email expressing her concern: would the Thai masseuses massage and milk my willy?

I wrote back:

Dear Lucy,

I know you are trying to resolve this awfully important life and death issue: Will she massage my willy?

My answer: No way will she, because the owner of the said willy is dead set against the massaging of willies, and he has even written a manifesto on the subject.

True, in Thailand, and in many other parts of the world, a section of masseuses, and about one-third of the Thai ones, will, at the psychologically appropriate time, conditions permitting, offer to massage their customers' lingams, digitally or orally, the major reason being that the tip skyrockets from around nothing or 20 per cent to a 100 to 300 per cent. And the reason I refuse is not because I think I can do it myself for no charge at all, and that God helps those that helps themselves, didn't good old Benjamin Franklin say so in *Poor Richard's Almanac*, etc. No, dearie, I'm a bit of a conservative, a bit of a Papist on this (the Pope and I disagree on most subjects, but this), and believe the holy lingam must be preserved for sacred emission only within the soft, wet and warm confines of the only friend it will ever have—the sacred yoni, as divine purpose intended it.

Actually, about half the Thai masseuses will respond to your 'No, thanks!' with greater respect for you ('Oh, you're a *good* man!' or something to that effect, which is not to say they think the other sorts immoral, but that they are neutral or understanding towards them). Whereas the other half will think of you as a stuck-up bastard or Cheap Charlie, and either look very disappointed or cast a pall of gloom on the surroundings. Or worse, they will take it out on you by giving you a bad massage in the remaining time available—which is why I sometimes pretend to delay my decision till the very end, hoping to keep them hoping. But then, the moment they begin to make their move, I try to make my position clear, or else, willy-nilly, I might find my willy in the manipulating hands of the masseuse. And once my willy has deserted to the enemy side (that is, to her side), it may be too late to protest—especially if she demands that I lodge the protest in triplicate.

Also, I don't intentionally patronize the obviously shady places. Shady or not, about one-tenth of Thai masseuses will nevertheless make a sneaky attempt to arouse you so as to change your mind. Still, I'm not a man of weak will power in this matter, and once they know they stand no chance, they give up.

As with the masseuse at the Regency Hotel: Bee gave me a good professional massage for forty-five minutes, and then, at the psychological moment, fifteen minutes before the conclusion, she asked, 'Want massage for ping pong?' I pretended not to understand, and not just because of the ping pong effect of the tip quadrupling. Though I wanted to ask, just for laughs, 'So will you massage my ping until it goes pong, or will you massage my dong until it goes ding?'

I know I could have invoked the fifth amendment and avoided answering your question, but I did answer it anyway, simply because it gave me sheer joy to write this email (and I can't say this about a lot of other emails). Indeed, anytime the subject is my willy, I'm more than willing to hold forth.

By the way, I don't mean to say I *never* did it. Did it a few times, long ago, out of curiosity—in other words, on a writer's need-to-know basis—or once or twice out of mere overpowering need. But not recently, because I feel it stands (verb chosen deliberately) no comparison to the 'real thing'. The real thing with you, for example.

Yours ever, etc. . . .

A

Unfortunately, my romantic connection with the intelligent and sweet but high-strung Lucy—who kissed passionately, fifteen minutes at a time, and who gave me high marks for my kissing, but left our lovemaking unrated, and whose plans for me included my bringing her *The New York Times* and breakfast every morning to her bed for the rest of her life—didn't last long after that too revealing email (please be advised, all of you men, that while confession may be good for the soul, and especially for the lapsed Catholic soul, it rarely is in a romantic relationship with a woman). Luckily for me though, she was soon replaced by a relaxed and easily risible twenty-five-year-old Thai who had never heard of *The New York Times*.

Until then, though, I had to ward off other Thai masseuses with dishonourable intentions towards my willy. As when in Bangkok where, at a new beauty salon near the Phrom Pong skytrain station, I stumbled upon a golden masseuse named Pao, who knew about fifty different ways to massage my bottom, all of them so gloriously tantalizing that I wanted her massage to go on forever. She seemed such a natural, as if massaging without even thinking about it, and if you were to ask her to repeat a particular move the next day, she would draw a blank.

I was touched by the kindness in her eyes and her soft smile. She is strong and larger than most Thais, which is probably why she has difficulty finding a sweetheart or a husband. She is twenty-nine and single and says she doesn't want to marry a Thai man because they drink a lot, gamble and take drugs.

In traditional (or ancient) Thai massages, which are far less sensuous and far more punishing, sometimes bordering on the sadistic and bone-crushing, especially if the masseuse is the female wrestler type, the primary objective is general body health, to be achieved by means of assisted yoga. But Pao's goal, as is the goal of 80 per cent of Thai women who give oil massages, is to excite the customer to such an intensity that he has no option but to go either for the digital penile yogic 'special'—in other words, the 'hand release', which is where the big tips come from—or the oral yogic special, or blow job, which will shower her with the biggest tips. I don't like specials, I tell Pao frankly. I would rather just fuck.

Like most things in life, however, not all specials are created equal.

To start with: hand specials, or the janata version of happy endings, simply aren't my thing, even though they can be quite pleasurable in the right hands. I can't say exactly why, and I don't think it's my puritanical nature. It is rather that I feel that a man at the conclusion of having been jacked off by a woman looks like a pretty sorry animal, sans dignity. Seconds after the orgasm, all he's got is a wet tool and a woman with wet fingers who is rushing off to wipe them (if she hasn't already prepared for this occasion with tissues) and to hand you tissues to do your own wiping sometimes. You are at this moment simply a mess who requires cleaning.

I turn down happy endings partly because I prefer ecstatic endings: real sex, when you come inside a woman, a woman you have helped raise to a plateau of joy, and there's a certain intimacy between you, a bond, a loving feeling, and you usually want to hold her, and she wants to hold you, and respects you and adores you . . . and probably exchanges cuddles and kisses and intimate conversation with you for some time thereafter. This is sublime and precious indeed, especially if you hold each other and don't immediately withdraw and rush to the bathroom to wash up. Usually, my post-orgasmic tool shrinks far more slowly when inside a loving, warm woman than if hurriedly pulled out or abandoned and left to the mercy of the elements.

Also, as I come much faster when someone's handling me digitally, and because, as you grow older, you don't spring back quite so quickly, this feels like a waste of God-given libido: So many women, so little time—how very true indeed, so why shrink further the potential time that you can spend with them?

A blow job, on the other hand, from the right kind of woman—with thick, sensuous lips, a sweet smile, genuine passion, a great head of hair that is loose, lavish, and whose ends are stimulating—while her mouth moves up and down and sideways—such a blow job can be divine. It also helps if your service provider has the right attitude and technique—and well-filed teeth. By attitude, I mean that I have to be convinced that for the woman, what she is doing is natural, pleasurable and a genuine part of her sensual nature—not something she is doing only for the money. As it happens, I confess I have succumbed to a handful (mouthful?) of offers of blow jobs in massage rooms, but on the whole, I prefer my oral sex to be part of a larger sensual experience that includes plenty of foreplay and real intercourse. A blowjob for the sake of a blowjob does not appeal to me, except for the first couple of years when it was still a novelty.

As foreplay alone, a sensual oil massage in Thailand, which can be had for as little as fifteen dollars, is unbeatable. A two-hour oil massage from a sexy Thai woman is like two hours of high-class foreplay. For me, foreplay, when done right, is by far the best part of making love, or at least equal in intensity and quality, when done right. Imagine getting two hours of foreplay from someone who is going to make love to you? It rarely happens in real life, except for the first couple of years of courtship and sex in a repressed country, and possibly for the first few months in a sexually liberal country. Which is why an oil massage from one of those sexy Thai bombshells is the bargain of a lifetime.

I have more recently heard of a specialized offering called the tantric lingam massage, which is far more sophisticated and complete than a 'hand job' or 'happy ending'. I would certainly have no objection to getting one of these every two weeks from a trained professional, though on other days I would rather prefer to conserve my mojo for the real thing: sublime boom boom.

11

LINGAM AND YONI MASSAGE: A SAFE SEX, ANTI-WAR AND ECONOMIC RECOVERY TOOL

Like Buddhism, lingam massage was invented in India, but you are far more likely to hear of it outside the country. I was completely unaware of it until I accidentally stumbled on the expanding great Filipino lingam massage debate.

That was when I discovered that professional lingam massage was something of an enviable and exclusive specialty, like cardiology, angioplasty, neurosurgery or rocket science. Not only was it an esoteric art practised by a few professionals (known in private circles as the priestesses of the holy rod), its very existence, like that of tantra (of which it is a part), was known only to a few connoisseurs.

First, to clear the air and explain what a lingam massage is *not*: it is *not* a dickie massage. Neither is it some variant of abusing the wicked stick, adjusting the antenna, beating the pud, burping the baby, choking the chicken, couch hockey for one, cranking the love pump, debugging the hard drive, greasing the three-legged cow, jerking the gherkin, or lubricating the love monkey. Or shaking your banana.

It's not the traditional happy ending either, though it may lead to a mind-bogglingly spiritual and transcendent happy ending.

So what *is* a 'professional lingam massage'—the kind that had the powerful Philippines Roman Catholic Church, led by its pink-capped generals, training its heavy artillery at some delicate and vulnerable Filipina belles? (The Philippines, a country with thousands of islands and spectacular beaches, is a country of great contradictions—with some of the hottest, sexiest women, who are outstanding kissers like Indonesian women, residing side by side with the ubiquitous presence of Catholicism and widespread opposition to legalized abortion.)

My undercover investigation revealed that while the West expends its fabled ingenuity in developing Star Wars defence systems, genetically modified eggplants and more scrumptious pigs, it is the East, places like Singapore, Malaysia and the Philippines, that concentrates on perfecting the art of living: for example, the gracious, noble and vital art and science of lingam massage, whose secrets, I now believe, ought to be deposited in a time capsule and buried in a deep, underground phallus-shaped vault for the benefit and happiness of future generations.

Thanks to the Internet, YouTube and jet aircraft, however, lingam massage may soon be as much a piece of our common planetary heritage as tea bags, Big Macs and Spiderman.

The website of Article Doctor explains: 'The tantra lingam massage is a *spiritual* tradition, which had its origin in India . . . about 4,000 years ago. Hence tantra can also be stated as a form of yoga.' Yoga to discipline the notoriously unruly male member, also known in various circles as the baby basher and the heat-seeking moisture missile? Now that makes sense—it's a no-boner! Though twenty years of solitary yogic meditation in the midst of the Sahara Desert on a diet of boiled brown rice and water blended with stale tofu might be a more effective strategy for taming the one-eyed monkey.

The website of White Lotus East is somewhat more explicit: 'The goal is to massage the lingam, also including testicles, perineum and sacred spot (prostate), externally, allowing the man to surrender to a form of pleasure he may not be accustomed to.'

Right, baby, count me in: around five years of daily practice should help me to get accustomed to this kind of pleasure.

While a video on YouTube says: 'It's about the *journey* . . .' (meaning orgasm is not the goal), adding that lingam massage can heal trauma and 'awaken your man's inner clitoris'.

Next stop: your man's inner G-spot. Followed by his inner vagina and his inner uterus.

As a man who had recently experienced a world of trauma and whose inner clitoris needed a healing jolt of greased lightning, I decided to investigate.

My informant is a fantasy novelist from the Philippines resort island of Cebu, where lingam massage was the explosive issue of early 2010, trumping global warming and Tiger Woods's multiple mistress scandal. He tells me his inner clitoris is throbbingly awake thanks to his visits to two local lingam massage joints named Authentic Lingam Massage and Chuva-Chuva. In Chuva-Chuva, he says, the masseuses dress like schoolgirls, and both joints offer 'a one-hour whole body massage plus lingam, all for P900'. Wow, that's less than the *tip* you'd have to pay for a plain old 'happy ending' in New York! It's what you might have to pay to simply take off your shirt at one of those forbidding Great American Shirted Back Rub joints.

Further, added my excited informant, 'In a hand job, they simply oil the organ and masturbate it (Ugh!). The lingam massage is more elaborate as it includes the thighs, testicles and other parts before the conclusive masturbation.' In other words, more bang-bang-bang for your buck.

Why do men need lingam massages? According to the website of White Lotus East, 'to learn to relax and to receive', and to 'experience their softer, more receptive side'—unlike their usual, goal-oriented mode. Whereas the website of the Filipino Lingam Massage Venture (displaying a photograph of a bevy of sultry beauties whom I would any day trust my lingam with) goes further: 'Men, being competitive, usually suffer from anxieties and frustrations. It is believed that they keep a lot of their stress in the abdomen and pelvic area.'

True, that's where I keep most of mine (except for the tiny bit that I hide inside my socks for emergencies), but glad to have an official, independent confirmation from an authoritative source. The site goes on to explain that its lingam specialists (all women—what a delightful coincidence) have been trained by a tantric priest based in Malaysia and Singapore. (Sadly, India, birthplace of tantra, is no place to hunt for a good lingam massage; you might get arrested merely for having made the mistake of *asking* for one. But, had it been otherwise, the chief tantric priest of the lingam massage division might have been titled Swami Lingacharya of Dickenballapuram Mutt.)

The Anti-War Consequences of Focused Pleasure

Returning to the delightful subject of inner clitorises: Now I truly believe if only many a world leader's inner clitoris—which is often in a coma—were to be kicked awake by some lingam massage expert, millions of lives could be saved by avoiding needless war.

If you are anti-war, you've no option but to be pro-lingam massage, the ultimate anti-war weapon. (Imagine T-shirts that proclaim 'Peaceniks for Lingam' or, 'Hell, No, We Won't Go . .without Lingam!'). Frequent lingam massages might have made of many a warlord a softer, gentler man who would not have recklessly dragged his nation into unjust, useless and unwinnable wars that destroy countries and people. For it has been repeatedly observed that men's fascination with guns, missiles and large, powerful gas-guzzling cars is a direct consequence of their quest for phallic substitutes to overcome their sexual frustration or their feelings of sexual inadequacy. (You know what I mean: the old male obsession with size matters.)

Therefore, I strongly suggest amending every national constitution to require that presidents and secretaries of defence undergo lingam or yoni massages twice every week in the interests of world peace. Lest I be accused of anti-yonist prejudice, I also suggest that men be compulsorily taught yoni massage in high school, so that when the legislatures and seats of government increasingly fill up with women, and when women become warlike (well, that's what the experts claim—that violence is an inevitable and gender-neutral outcome of power), men can pacify them with massages.

Behind the Philippines' explosive lingam massage debate—as polarizing an issue as health care reform in the US—lies the country's dual colonial history and mixed cultural ancestry: liberal, relaxed Southeast Asian island culture and genes warring against the colonial legacy of a morally uptight Catholic religion and hellfire, blah blah.

The crux of the debate: Does lingam massage promote health, and if so (or if not), is it immoral? Do we *have* to choose between spa heaven and God's heaven, or could we perhaps visit them on alternate evenings?

Cebu's Cardinal Vidal, joining calls to investigate spas offering 'indecent' services to their clients, has declared: 'Because they promote immorality, they should be stopped.'

But how can a *spiritual* practice promote immorality? And why is the cardinal taking such a hard stand against a therapeutic procedure that could avert prostate cancer? Why is he angry with those lovely prostate milkers, milkmaids doubling as Florence Nightingales? Still, city councillors, possibly prodded by the cardinal's displeasure, asked the Cebu City Anti-indecency Board to investigate if 'lingam massage' joints were indeed involved in 'indecent and lewd practices'.

In the same newspaper (*Cebu Daily News*), however, columnist Ricky Poca has accused men of using lingam massage for one thing only. I quote:

> The advertisement says lingam massage is good for the prevention of prostate cancer but many of its customers are young men. It's a hit . . . because it provides tremendous pleasure for men without having to engage in sexual intercourse.

> Personally I think it should be [investigated]. What lingam offers is simply sexual pleasure, although I know that some men welcome it. For them, they are engaging in safe sex, not necessarily therapy against prostate cancer.

Should massage be investigated because it gives pleasure? If so, why not also investigate beer, music and sunsets, all of which also provide pleasure? Nevertheless, I hail his column's positive implications: that lingam massage is a stone that nails two birds—prostate cancer as well as STDs and AIDS! Indeed, an NGO's or philanthropist's wet dream!

Admittedly, the lingam massage trend could upset many a woman—girlfriends, wives, and perhaps just lonely women looking for a warm tumble in the hay—who would be left to fend for themselves by men whose inner clitoris is in seventh heaven. But so long as it is in the interests of safe sex, one of the holy icons of the modern age, why object to it? Well, of course, they are going to object to any procedure in which they get left out, so why not also offer free or discount yoni massages to the women who are complaining?

Meanwhile, at the website of sunstar.com.ph, lingam advocate Lorenzo Ninal fumes at Filipino puritanism:

> Because ours is a culture that finds certain innocent words referring to some parts of our anatomy 'obscene'.
>
> The words I am referring to are penis, genitals, orgasm, ejaculation, masturbation, and other terms that *you, with your puritan upbringing, wish did not exist at all.*

But they exist, after all, these wondrous gifts of God to humankind, so one might as well grow up, right?

Meanwhile, Cebu's police chief, under attack from the puritans, explained that 'the police have to catch a masseuse in the act of doing something indecent before they can take action'. (I would gladly join the police force if assigned to this job, and promise not to accept kickbacks—well, at least not in cash.)

While in the *Cebu Daily News*, Honey Yoo, owner of Authentic Lingam Massage, defended her service as a widely accepted 'wellness' massage. 'It is accepted in strict Singapore and widely embraced in Muslim Malaysia, practised in Egypt, Thailand, New York, California and London,' Yoo said. Fair enough: what's good enough for Singaporeans and New Yorkers is good enough for us.

But Yoo goes further and uses globalization and competitiveness to make her pro-lingam case, urging openness to new ideas and asking, 'How will we become globally competitive if we ... judge and mislead our customers?'

Why not go even further? I suggest that lingam massage be used not just as a tool for safe sex, world peace and the prevention of prostate cancer, but also as a means to global economic recovery. In just the last four years, the world has lost around $5–10 trillion in pointless wars, dangerous and fantastically expensive weapons systems (male toys), and the destruction of the financial system caused by men playing around with other people's lifetime savings. Specifically, by whom? Just a few thousand bankers, brokers and financial players in New York, London and a few other financial capitals. The solution: a law requiring all financial workers to submit themselves to a one-hour lingam (or yoni) massage every morning, between 10 a.m. and 11 a.m.

It is only after the traders and bankers have been drained of their hostility, excess sperm, and their immense lust for cash that they would be permitted to show up for work. Landing up at their offices around noon, they may indulge in half an hour of good-humoured trading or bank business before heading out for their three-Martini, tax-deductible lunches. Returning at 3 p.m., they could do another hour of friendly trading and servicing the share accounts of senior citizens before returning home to be dutiful husbands and fathers.

Consider the savings:

From banks and entire European countries that don't have to be bailed out: $2 trillion

From Wall Street firms that don't have to be bailed out: $2 trillion

From cuts in defence budgets worldwide: $2 trillion

Improved productivity from better education: $1 trillion

Reduced policing costs resulting from a big post-lingam fall in violent crime: $1 trillion

Imagine what the world could do with $8 trillion each year—new jobs created, roads, schools and hospitals built, potential terrorists sent to schools for less than the $200 million cost of the optional air-conditioning system, stereo and leather seats on a $500 million B-1 bomber . . .

That's $8 trillion for a world population of seven billion; even if half of it is used to improve infrastructure and give free medical care, the rest can be distributed to us common people, and it is still not something to sneeze at.

Not to sneeze at either is the great boost to gross national happiness and employment (all those new lingam-specialist jobs, training institutes and lingam massage parlours giving jobs to the construction industry), coupled with cuts in police forces, prison and military spending . . . thus balancing national budgets across the world.

Add to the above a lowered crime rate and a kinder, gentler humanity: it's nothing but win, win, win.

And now to remedy this chapter's tilt towards lingams, I would like to devote the rest to yonis. I am all for women's empowerment through yoni massage. You can't leave nearly half of the world's population out of any solution to the world's problems, and as women are increasingly better represented in many of the most important professions, one must fully recognize their importance.

The website of White Lotus East says: 'Yoni is the Sanskrit word for the vagina that is loosely translated as "sacred space" or "sacred temple". In tantra, the yoni is seen from a perspective of love and respect. This is particularly important for men to learn.'

I say: Amen. Count me in. I am an eternal worshipper at the said temple, and my love and respect for the yoni (or what E.L. James calls the inner goddess) is boundless as the expanding universe, which, by the way, is nothing but scientific jargon for the cosmic yoni. Not only do I volunteer my services (giving one free yoni massage a week, my gesture of giving back what the world of women has given to me), I urge inclusion of the right to yoni massage as a sub-clause of the UN Charter's universal right to massage.

But are they legal in most countries, including India? Otherwise, I suggest their inclusion in the constitution. If made legal, I suspect that very soon, some enterprising businessman will start a chain of franchised establishments called the Great Indian (or American) Pussy Rub, which could become the next big thing after Microsoft and Google.

It really is time for the yoni anti-defamation league to take a strong stand and steamroller over all obstacles to yoni massage.

What about the Eastern hemisphere? Despite the Filipino brouhaha over the rise of lingam massage in Cebu, my Filipino source, when asked whether the poor, oppressed yoni was getting its share, replied, 'Not really.'

This is a grave injustice, one that we shall not take lying on our backs. There's no other alternative but for women's groups to march across the planet (a movement which could be named 'Yonis across the World', with the theme song '*And justice for all yonis*', starring Gal Pacino (?)) and demand compulsory yoni massage for all women, from the ages of eleven to sixty. If yoni massage were freely and widely offered, women would be more empowered and less easily enslaved; besides which, I am not only against wars fought with guns and bombs, but also the endless wars between the sexes, which rob humanity of so much of the energy we could devote to more crucial causes such as mosquito nets, cheap medicines and better nutrition for Third World children, and of course, global warming. Frequent yoni massages would leave us less inclined towards participating in such internecine wars.

How can such a massive change be achieved? Perhaps if the major powers of the world launched a Yoni Massage Corps to serve the cause of women's empowerment in Third World countries, and also change the United Nations laws so that the International Court of Justice would, if necessary, hold world leaders down while they were being administered their compulsory lingam (or yoni) massages.

To conclude with an ancient Sumerian poem, which reflects a timeless question that must always be a consideration in matters of social, national and intercontinental policy:

> As for me, Inanna,
> Who will plow my vulva?
> Who will plow my high field?
> Who will plow my wet ground?

Yes, indeed. So long as the world is blessed with vulvas, some three billion of them and rising at last count, someone or the other will have to plow them—or failing this onerous and crucial task (which ought to be added to the Millennium Development Goals), at least *massage* them.

12

SOUTHEAST ASIAN MASSAGE VARIATIONS

Following my divorce and after losing my children to the machinations of the law, I tried to drown my sorrow, or numb it to stupefaction, with Bangkok's multifarious culinary offerings, lots of lemon-steamed fresh white snapper, dancing shrimp and prawn fried rice. At other times, I would seek refuge in the white sands of the island of Koh Samui. Here, massages were my points of connection with the locals, whose language was profoundly strange to me. Indeed, it was only six months after I had made ecstatic love to a lush-haired and buxom young woman named Nam that I learned that 'nam' is the Thai word for water—a word I ought to have picked up in my first month. Whereas I only had to walk into a massage shop and say 'massage', and not a word more, and within minutes I would find myself naked or nearly naked and horizontal, having my touch-starved body comforted by the silky fingers of a smiling Thai girl.

Sometimes, it wasn't even necessary to say the word 'massage'. A girl sitting at the door of the shop would smile at you, read your mind, grab your hand, and simply drag you in, while the other girls watched and laughed. And, despite your weak protests that you were actually on your way to get lunch, you would find yourself on a massage table or bed, surrendering to dictatorially enforced pain relief, pleasure and heaven. (Heck, it would have been easier to resist the Nazi SS.)

Body Massage versus Soul Massage

For many years, I was foxed by the signs, in parts of Thailand, advertising 'Body Massage'. What does it mean? *Body* massage as opposed to *soul* massage? Could one go in for a combo package: some body massage, and some soul massage? And shouldn't a good body massage automatically do some good to the soul?

It was only later that I discovered that the 'body massage', often offered by touts with a leer and a wink, was a full frontal type of 'body-to-body' massage in which a pneumatic masseuse applied oil onto her naked body, the front of it at least, and then moved her body, especially her breasts, up and down your nude front and back in what was a multi-pronged assault of pleasure. Thus, a 'body massage' is roughly one half of a sandwich massage, but without the soap, bubbles, plastic float and general insanity that accompanies the latter. Obviously, the therapists cannot be too thin or underdeveloped, or there would be little pleasure for the man, and not much good for his soul either, unless he were a Calvinist. I would even venture that prominent nipples add at least 27.3 per cent to the pleasure of a body massage, whereas inverted nipples are an immediate disqualification.

I hear it on good authority that there are now a few Manipuris who offer this massage in Bangalore; but in the late nineties or early 2000s, you could have been sentenced to life imprisonment for merely *thinking* about such a massage in India.

The Ah-Soul Massage

Not only do good massages benefit body and soul, but in the right hands, they might also do good to your ah-soul—as an Indonesian woman put it (arsehole I mean, also asshole or butthole, as the Americans call it)—or the lowest depression in the valley between your bottom cheeks. This was one of the great techniques in the erotic arsenal of Kissanee of Chanthaburi.

Kissanee, who is such a bundle of joy and laughter, and who twice had joyous sex with me, invests her whole body and soul into her massages. She lets her soft-oiled fingers graze your bottom line with a feather-light and endearing touch, both during the upward movement—which also glazes over the back of the balls and sometimes the back of your cock, peeping out from between your legs—and, once again, during the downward movement starting from the top of your buttocks. These strokes are excruciatingly pleasurable, and each time her hand roams over my bottom line, my cock shoots out an extra quarter inch, then shrinking likewise until one more stroke makes it stretch again.

Ancient Massage versus Modern Massage

And what about those signs in some Eastern countries which advertise 'ancient' massage? The definition varies from country to country, but if it is an 'ancient' Thai massage, it generally means you keep your pants or underpants on. The word 'ancient' simply gives the massage a traditional and cultural respectability—the tradition is to wear the loose pyjamas and shirt they provide you, which are quite similar to the clothes you wear when practising judo. But if privacy permits, and if you think that any massage without skin-on-skin contact is missing the essence of massage, you might try *bargaining* to take them off, as I have occasionally done. Whereas with a Swedish or Thai oil massage, you take off your pants and everything else right at the beginning, so that nothing comes between you, your 'election', and the masseuse (though the Westernized or prudish places may cover you with a small towel, to be lifted or reached under when necessary). At which point, the only remaining task is to bargain to have the masseuse take *her* clothes off. (In Thailand, any and every combination is potentially up for sale. For the right price, you could even have an elephant brought into the massage room.)

The Jaybird Massage

Which brings me to what I call the jaybird massage. I kick myself when I think of the five hundred or so massages I have had in the East in which I could have had the masseuse nude during the entire massage for just a few dollars more, but failed to act decisively and early, partly because of my shyness and partly because of the fear of rejection. On the rare occasions when I did act, often just ten minutes before the conclusion, emboldened by my arousal or the masseuse's friendliness and, perhaps, horniness, I would be surprised at how little the woman required to be persuaded to let her skin breathe and to have her pussy and ass released from their confinement within suffocating nylon panties.

The Joint Shower Massage

However, in one Bangkok establishment next to the Thong Lo skytrain station, between shopkeepers selling brown roast ducks with defeated expressions on their faces, no bargaining was needed—the masseuse, quite gorgeous with a tall and lovely figure, a woman with the clean and wholesome looks of your sister or your rich cousin, stripped unasked right at the beginning, in all her splendiferous young, tight nudity. It turned cut this was a practical measure to join me in the shower, a glass-walled enclosure within the massage room, which was a soundproof cabin in the basement obviously designed to muffle the customer's screams of pleasure (or pain, as the case may be). Her purpose was plainly an altruistic one: to help me soap myself all over (and being a gallant and chivalrous chap, I returned the favour), and to also wash herself in the bargain. For Thai women are fabulously clean and will shower at the least excuse, from five to ten times a day, while also despising civilizations where regular bathing is a rarity. But perhaps the girl's chief design was to make me feel so aroused from being near to, and being bumped into by, her gloriously naked, soapy body, that I would agree to full sex—which would be a piffling 1,500 baht extra. Isn't it amazing how few of us realize that in giving we shall get, that generosity is one of the fundamental energizers of the human race?

The Sleeping on Chest Massage

One of the most delightful examples of how relaxed things are in Thailand and Indonesia (and when the masseuse is relaxed, it helps you relax; if she is uptight, your muscles clench, no matter how technically proficient her strokes): Once, a Thai masseuse stopped right in the middle of the massage to announce, 'I am tired', and leaned her head on my chest affectionately to rest it there for a few minutes. Returning her affection (or else, possibly, I was concerned that she might fall asleep!)—I hadn't known her since I met her thirty minutes back—I fondled her hair and massaged her shoulders and back, even as her head rested on my chest. This is how relaxed the relationship can get—boundaries be damned, and lawsuits for 'inappropriate behaviour' or 'sexual harassment' laughed out of court and off the front pages of newspapers.

The other semi-sleeping-on-chest massage was by a horny thirty-five-year-old who wanted me to be her boyfriend. She lay her head on my chest, facing my left arm, as she massaged my upper right arm and shoulder. The erotic advantage of that, to me, was that her cheek was in full contact with my left nipple, which made a thousand pleasure neurons scream with joy, while her gorgeously thick head of hair falling over the entire eastern portion of my chest, like the Icelandic volcano cloud spreading over the whole of western Europe, sent indescribable sensations of ecstasy tingling through my skin. Naturally, I forgave her her horniness, as well as her dishonourable intentions. After all, I am not a man entirely above reproach.

The Play with Hair and Tits Massage

Now for the play with hair and tits massage. In Nakhon Ratchasima—a town that is the gateway to north-eastern Thailand and the region of Isaan, which produces more masseuses per capita than any other region in the world—the masseuse was not only good, she showed her appreciation of me by pulling at one or two of my chest hairs playfully. In return, I showed my appreciation by placing my hand gently on her breast—at which she gave me the kind of playful 'slap on the hand' that you give a two-year-old to tell him he is being naughty. It was done with a smile, almost with the unspoken preface that boys will be boys—and it didn't necessarily mean that she didn't want a repetition; it was just part of the ritual, the dance, which could lead to anything. Indeed, she invited me to return the next day, whereupon she allowed me to lift her blouse and look at her breasts with their large chocolate nipples, which I told her were beautiful. Forty-seven years old, in Thailand, in a massage joint where youth was worshipped and rewarded, my compliment probably meant a lot more to her than money.

Long before I had started to play with her breasts, I had started to fondle and play with her hair, once removing her hair clip to let her glorious mane fall down her back. After watching me bemusedly for a while, she had replaced the clip, complaining it was hot. But the next day, she loosened her hair of her own accord just for my benefit. On this occasion, I also played with her curvaceous ass, her soft yet well-sculpted buttocks. That I could do this without even the playful mock punishment of a soft slap was one of the great gifts of Thailand and some parts of Southeast Asia, for the ass was the female asset with the least taboo, and it made me glad to be far, far away from 'civilization'.

The Sexual Ballet Massage

Often, in this particular Southeast Asian country, the massage, even if there's not a single overtly sexual act in it, assumes the form of a sexual ballet, dance or tango, and therefore can be marvellously arousing—imagine fifty shades of sexual arousal without a single moment of actual penetration.

All of this usually happens in a massage place or spa, well-furnished and almost classy, with massage rooms in which mattresses are spread out on the floor. Spotless white silk bed sheets with a pink silk decorative drape cover the mattresses, and a flower, a real flower, is left on the pillow as an advance token of the masseuse's love. The room is often perfumed, and the lighting is low and romantic.

The customer lies down on the mattress, nude under a towel, or sometimes with loose and thin shorts provided by the establishment. These shorts are, in practice, often optional for foreigners, who have special privileges due to their 'ignorance', or pretended ignorance, of local customs; or perhaps they can claim to be too big—big in all senses—to fit into the little shorts or pyjamas they have been provided with. (It is generally—though often erroneously—assumed by the locals that visitors from foreign, non-East Asian countries are monstrously endowed.)

So here the horny foreign customer waits, tingling with expectation; he awaits the arrival of the masseuse, who he has selected after a quick viewing, or sometimes is not aware of the existence of until the moment she actually arrives. It is this tremulous anticipation of the mystery woman who will spend an hour with you, sometimes in a closed room, or in a partly open room, but with you alone—the anticipation itself is an exquisite pleasure.

And often it turns out that the masseuse who arrives, like a gift sent by God, fresh from Heaven, is pretty, smiling, between twenty and twenty-five, and seemingly at peace with the world. She has just been watching television, joking and indulging in horseplay with her friends, and there is a light blush on her face. And you are so delighted to be so near her for the next one hour, at your service and for your pleasure, that you are willing to forgive her even if she knows not the first thing about massage. When she arrives, she will smile, bend gracefully and at some point lift your sheet or towel and 'rearrange' it—in the process, possibly getting a quick peep of what lies underneath.

Besides which, she is often as aroused, hot and wet between her legs by this prospect of discovering a new man. And she laughs easily, for she finds the world to be a funny place, and also finds you, her customer, a little amusing. For example, the fact that you might have a long nose, or big eyes, unlike the men in her family or village. Like someone she has seen in the movies, perhaps.

On the mattress, as she 'gets into bed' with you, clothed, though often in shorts, not only are her hands soft, her skin brushes against yours in a thousand different ways, mindboggling in their variety, causing a million electrical charges to rush through your body (few of these infinite number of erotic combinations you will find listed in those profusely illustrated massage books by Western authors designed for Western therapists).

Two of these positions deserve special mention.

The first is one in which, as she massages your chest or back, her whole body alternately advances towards and retreats from you, the rhythm mimicking the up and down movement of a woman on top in a classy X-rated movie, a woman riding a man and enjoying every moment of it. Often, if she is reaching for your upper arm while seated on your buttocks or lower back, her breasts may bump onto your back, or chest, and you'd have to be dead or pretty thick-skinned not to enjoy the rush of blood. A leap of joy in that tiny part of you that is waiting for just such a moment.

The second position is one in which she actually straddles your bum or your waist, though she is fully clothed and your waist is covered with a towel. If you are face down, the towel often rides down, and there are moments when you can feel the warmth of her soft and spongy vulva, covered by pretty thin material, bumping against your naked buttocks. She is assuming this position for ergonomic purposes, of course, it being the most energy-efficient way for her to massage your entire upper back with both hands. But if someone were to observe just your silhouettes from behind a screen, they might think something far wilder is going on: that she is wearing a strap-on dildo and having anal sex with you!

Another innocent but highly erotic move, to me, is when the masseuse sits cross-legged on the mattress or on the floor beside you, and is massaging your arm, and lets your hand rest on her bare or lightly covered thigh—for support. Ah, soft thigh—sometimes, your long fingers may even, in the course of *her* movements, touch her groin or her mons veneris, and she doesn't seem to mind or even notice—such is the beautiful concentration with which she is massaging you. At this point, you might be greatly provoked to tickle the clitoris with one finger. And she would respond either by laughing, or by laughing as well as giving your hand a playful, soft slap. Of course, you may not do it at all, but the very thought that you could so easily gives you a hard-on, and meanwhile, something is rising between your legs … and do you really believe she doesn't notice?

This is the kind of freakily aphrodisiac massage that often leaves me so aroused that when it is over, I desperately need to have sex, which I didn't when I entered the massage establishment—in fact, I may even have been worrying about my lack of sexual desire.

Most often, in this country, the masseuses in the 'legitimate' massage establishments will almost *never* have sex with you. A lot of them return home to their village or small town for three- to five-day vacations during all the major national holidays; on one such visit, they will find a man and become hitched for life. So, aroused by the nubile but unavailable masseuse, I will end up having sex with someone else, a bank of fuckable friends that I have to call in for help with a sexual emergency; at other times, I may not find such help, and decide to go to bed and have a bad night's sleep.

But I'm not complaining. Things could be a lot, lot worse, a helluva lot worse. The country that I was in could have been Saudi Arabia.

The Triple Massage in Bali

From the noisy, brassy, sluttish city of Thai angels, Bangkok, I flew into Bali a couple of days after Christmas, and settled down in the magical and hypnotic seaside town of Sanur, where I was delighted to discover that it was the mango season, and juicy mangoes were being sold for a song by big-breasted Balinese hawkers.

Unlike the wild and roaring, tourist-packed Kuta on the west coast, Sanur is a peaceful, idyllic beach town on the south-eastern coast of the island, washed by the gentle waves of the Bali Sea lapping the shore like quiet, understated music. The town itself seems to have come from another century—sculptured houses, walls and gates, exquisitely artistic and lush gardens and courtyards, and temples. This delicate, tasteful town sent me into a contemplative mood—I missed my children and the comforts of the past.

Bali in January is drenched by the monsoon downpours, but this hardly dampens the spirits of the natives, for whom water is a primary element, filling up pools and fountains, making puddles in the street, and causing the ubiquitous fish to celebrate. In the rainy season, green Bali is usually greener, and one must watch out for slippery or mossy patches on the hard Balinese stone, which is everywhere—in pavements, steps and courtyards. And walking up Sanur's main street one day during an afternoon break from the rains, I spotted the signboard of the Queen's Beauty Clinic.

Here I learned, for the first time, of the triple massage, which my battered and hungry soul couldn't resist—because the advertised price for six soft, young and delightfully ticklish hands (or thirty fingers) was an irresistible seven dollars, or just slightly above one dollar per hand.

The women had shoulder-length black hair, soft and sensuous, and like most Balinese women wore bright red lipstick, of a red fuck-me colour, and loose blouses in which their breasts breathed easily, and their every movement could be observed.

Unlike the Thai sandwich massage, in the usual double or triple massage, there is no soap or plastic float, and there are no naked women. What makes this different from a regular massage is that the professional manpower or womanpower has been doubled or tripled, so that four or six hands are massaging you simultaneously.

I was soon horizontal on a table, my pelvic danger zone fig-leaved with a small towel, while Ketut, the owner, and her two young employees, Rai and her friend, girls of eighteen or nineteen wearing thin cotton Balinese sarongs (the Balinese sarong is such a delightful and nakeder-than-naked garment, far more arousing and vulnerable than jeans or saris), had their soft hands, like warm little newborn puppies, wriggling up and down my back as if they had been made by their creator for precisely this purpose. The first session was wild; for while the girls themselves were quite well-behaved, my senses rocked and partied with grossly unearned and undeserved sybaritic overstimulation (on the other hand, I didn't deserve some of the other stuff that had happened to me either—so there must be some balancing providence out there).

The next time, only the two young girls worked on me. I told them that in the US, it was the practice to massage the whole body, including the buttocks. So Rai obliged, so efficiently and sensuously that it had the effect I was hoping it wouldn't—it was lucky they didn't notice.

Ah, their innocence—these girls seemed so innocent in the way they negotiated around my erection and sometimes laughed at it. It was an innocence that was both touching and excruciatingly arousing.

Other than that, what is a double or triple massage like? You don't want to do it too often, only perhaps annually or semi-annually as a novelty and a variation, say in honour of Bill Clinton's birthday or International Women's Day. Though logically one would think that by doubling the workforce, one could halve the time taken, it doesn't quite work that way, and the double trouble saves only ten or fifteen minutes at most, while triple massage is in no way distinguishable in sensation from a double massage except in the elegant beauty of the number three.

In fact, much of the pleasure of a massage comes from being wholly focused on just one part of your body and noticing how it is being touched, soothed, aroused, the blood flowing into your painful zones and relieving your sore muscles, and sometimes being redirected into areas where the outcome could only be subversive. But this focus gets distracted when two or more different parts of your body are sending you somewhat different nerve-stimulation messages at the same time. Because no two pairs of hands or touches can ever be the same, every masseuse having her unique fingerprint or touch print, so to speak. As a result, by some weird mathematical formula, the two or three different sources of pleasure or therapeutic stimulation nearly cancel each other out.

And yet you can't help feeling a certain wonder, a certain sense of awe and regal, luxurious satisfaction at being so indulged in and pleasured by two young women, their four soft hands serving you and only you. It's partly an intellectual thrill to realize that you, poor sod, who has been so touch-starved in the past, is suddenly being showered with attention by two nubile females. It is as divine as a special blessing from the Dalai Lama, a rare sensation comparable to what a California group called the Human Awareness Institute describes as a shower of love, in which half-a-dozen people touch you and feel you with their hands at the same time. While the therapeutic reduction of pain and increased circulation also happens in a double or triple massage, it is only a side-benefit of so much movement and manipulation, and not the chief focus of it. Because I believe that the therapeutic reduction of pain occurs through consciousness: first the focus on the pain, then on its release, and then on the absence of pain. And when six lovely hands are running like hyperactive bunnies up and down your nude body, pain relief is not likely to be the top item on your list of priorities.

The Nyoman Massage

If you've visited Bali, there is a 25 per cent chance you have received the Nyoman massage, but never realized it, because nearly one-fourth of all Balinese men and women are named Nyoman (or Koman), meaning they happen to be the third child of their parents. Twenty days after my arrival there, I find myself in Candidasa, a quiet beach and temple town north-east of Sanur, with painted boats with blue sails in the distance, and the occasional lean boatman rowing a Buddha-fat Western tourist. A rocky island on the south-eastern horizon lazes under a veil of mist, while on the western horizon, Bali's presiding sacred mountain Gunung

Agung rises majestically, its calm façade belying its hot volcanic interior, quiet for now, but far from dead. It is late morning, sunny, and I'm already feeling horny thinking of my impending massage with Nyoman, who had met me earlier in the day and held my hands in hers for a long, long time, as if she were meeting a long-lost beloved or friend (such an unexpected gift of love and intimacy that it raised my erotic temperature by about a hundred degrees, which was the last thing I needed at that point when I was already at boiling temperature—but heck, who's going to refuse a gift?).

Also, she asked me if I was a sendiri, or travelling alone—when an Indonesian woman asks a man that question, it usually means that she has designs for him. Well, so what, I think at that moment, my penis doing most of the thinking for me. Damn it, massages are all about sex, and why not? Life is short! Fuck it, even if it has taken me eighteen years into my massage obsession to learn this.

And yet, wait a moment. Nothing is *all* about sex! Even sex is not all about sex. Sex is a programme of the species, and it's about connection with another human being, the search for a soul mate, for excitement and life. Every time I honour sex, I honour the goddess Venus (or the yoni goddess, if you will). So to all the idiots in my lives who have ever said to me, 'You *only* think about sex', I now issue a resounding 'Boo!' to their microscopic, tight-assed brains! They lack understanding, and they insult the cosmic yoni that created them.

Other variations offered by Bali's glorious spas include the mandi lulur massage—which is an exfoliating and body polishing massage using a paste of sandalwood, turmeric, groundnuts, rice and other scented woods, followed by a hot shower and the application of a yoghurt mix—and massages in which, for part of the time, your body is scrubbed with milk or immersed in a tub full of rose petals, often by female staff who are Javanese, not Balinese (I have invariably found Javanese women, including the Madurese, to be among the world's sexiest, far outshining most of their island neighbours including, sorry, the Balinese; besides which, their names so often have Indian roots, which gives me both a feeling of comfort and of glorious illicit pleasure—names like Ratna, Hapsari, Dewi, Ratih, Lakshmi, Sundari, Sari and Shakti). Cheap by Western standards, some of these massages can be quite expensive by Indonesian standards, and I myself nearly always chose the cheapest no-frills massage joints, where if the masseuse went well beyond the call of duty, I felt the indescribable emotional satisfaction of knowing that I had been the beneficiary of her generosity and sexuality, the beauty of her personality, and the beginnings of that warm feeling called love—and that my tiny payment had nothing to do with it. This realization was as much of a turn-on as the massage itself.

In most of these Southeast Asian countries, pure massages are abundant (it's much, much harder in China, where the recent social liberalization has resulted in an explosion of sexual availability, but not as much of real massage). And in the heavily touristed areas like Bali, the culture having reinvented itself partly to serve the wealthy Western tourist, massages run a wide gamut, from the sandy massages given by steel-fingered, hardy peasant women on Kuta Beach for as little as three dollars an hour, to the sophisticated massages in joints smelling of flowers and incense where beautiful young women fit to be kings' consorts massage you for eight dollars an hour and above.

However, it is a general rule that in countries like Thailand and Indonesia, if a relatively healthy man asks a taxi driver to take him to a massage place, the taxi driver will nearly always take him to the shady places—not just because of the near certainty of his getting a commission from the joint itself, but also because of the general assumption that if you are a reasonably healthy male between eighteen and fifty years, your overwhelming need is to get fucked (or perhaps they can read the urgency in your face, and gauge exactly how much in need of a good fuck you are). Double that conviction for foreign males, who are believed to be either constitutionally hornier than locals, or sex-starved, or both. I don't wish to pretend that I was above fucking—after all, these were the years just after my divorce, and I was pretty virile at the time, and tried to soothe my emotional pain and emptiness with both real massages as well as loads of fucking, often with women who were pretty horny themselves and always appreciated a good lover, a lover who filled them and took care of their entire bodies instead of coming and going in a heaving rush.

Besides, words are simply representations of meanings or concepts, and in different contexts and cultures, they represent different things. Over the years, travelling in various countries, I have realized that a massage is not supposed to mean, necessarily, a massage, but often is a euphemism for a broader range of services. Indeed, even after I picked up some of the local language, I would be frustrated in my attempts to obtain a decent massage at some massage joint, and ended up getting an enormously probing massage at a few. Sometimes, hurting badly and unable to find an obviously purely massage joint, I would show up at the dubious place and plead, 'I want *only* a massage please.' They would assign you a woman, for they don't want to turn away your business. But then, the assigned masseuse would resent you for not asking for more; she would keep inciting you to change your mind, hoping to earn the higher fee ...

13

WACKY MASSAGES IN CHINA AND ELSEWHERE

The Chinese Oh-You Massage

My first massage during my first and only visit to China was in Kunming, a city of broad boulevards at an altitude of 5,000 feet in south-western China, surrounded by tea plantations. In China, the food is so fresh, so authentic, so varied in its flavours, so reasonably priced—dumplings, Peking duck, seafood hot pot with noodles, pregnant fish—it makes all your senses come alive, but sooner rather than later, you will need a massage, for the mattresses tend to be very thin and somewhat hard. And, walking into a spa-cum-massage joint, an independent wooden building next to my hotel, I was given a locker key by the male receptionist and commanded by the male locker attendant (who looked like a People's Army veteran minus the uniform and the bayonet) to strip and change into a laughably brief pair of shorts. He then directed me to head into the steam and massage section, where the women, dressed like nurses in white uniforms, lay in wait to ambush me.

I had paid for the basic massage—around fifty yuan. And, glad to be relieved of my tight shorts, I lay naked under a towel as the masseuse began to massage me.

She didn't speak a word of English, or so I believed, and I not a word of useful Chinese, so we resigned ourselves to our respective roles in the massage, to take it as it came.

But around fifteen minutes into the massage, the woman, possibly thirty and passably pretty and nice-figured, began exclaiming, 'Oh you! Good!' every thirty seconds.

'Oh you! Good!' she kept saying, as I looked at her, mystified, thinking perhaps that the sight of my virile body was giving her an orgasm every thirty seconds (ah, my silly male ego!), and that while the 'Oh you!' was an orgasmic exclamation, the 'Good!' was a comment on the quality of the orgasm.

Only after thirty minutes of this did I finally figure out that 'Oh-you' was her Chinese pronunciation of 'oil'—which, with its two syllables, including the difficult 'l' sound, was too difficult for some Chinese to pronounce. All along, she had been urging me to change my massage to an *oil* massage, which she was better at, and for which her earnings and tips were higher. And also because the 'Oh you!' massage was much likelier to culminate in a happy ending for my little emperor.

I soon learned that if there is a lesson here in China, it's that illegal pleasure is going to have severe consequences . . . at least on your wallet. A Chinese massage ('health massage') costs from thirty to fifty yuan. But an oil massage is anything from 100 to 200 yuan. It's not the extra cost of the oil, but the promise of illicit titillation, of your skin being touched, perhaps sensuously, by a masseuse. Though things are changing, the official line still frowns on sensual pleasure. Wealth, yes; pleasure, no.

In between the austere 'Chinese health massage' and the decadent 'oil massage', there are a few other offerings in which you are permitted to discard one item of clothing, and the price climbs up for each item of clothing you are permitted to take off. If you *want* to take off your clothes, that is.

The problem with this system is that the constant pressure on you to go for more disturbs and spoils your pleasure and relaxation, which is the reason you have come to get a massage in the first place. It is like being assaulted non-stop by an insurance salesman while listening to a concert of the Berlin philharmonic orchestra.

In modern, far more cosmopolitan and fashionable Shanghai, in a quiet middle-class neighbourhood perhaps five miles away from the city centre with its futuristic skyscrapers, I received a reasonably competent massage from a thirty-year-old call-in masseuse who confessed to me that she was looking for a white man to give her a baby ('because the baby would be more intelligent'). Afterwards I discovered an ordinary-looking massage parlour, a small business, a house with around four rooms and six masseuses of different ages from twenty-two to forty-five. Once I entered my assigned room, the laughing twenty-two-year-old masseuse with gorgeous black hair jumped with great alacrity at the opportunity to substitute her initial offer of a happy ending with an all-out fuck, and seemed pretty grateful at the end of it. And so was I, because by then, I had been sex-starved for two weeks, and had come a long way from my sanctimonious hypocrisy of New York. It turned out to be a gorgeous, passionate, though not too-long, fuck, and she invited me for a return visit; I obliged, the next day. Two fucks in two weeks in a country of 1.3 billion people: a droplet in a vast ocean, but it humanized my visit, did something for international understanding and peace, and made up for my less-than-perfect satisfaction with the massages I had received in Kunming.

Hole-in-the-Door Massage

A friend of mine, who is more of an aficionado of sex than of massage, once visited a Phnom Penh massage joint which offered a choice from between a hundred masseuses, many of them young and pretty. And these were the kinds of masseuses who looked more like they liked to work with their pussies than with their hands. So he chose a masseuse, and the pair headed off to a room with only one thing on his mind: to have sex. In such places, you enter a room, close the door, and during the rest of the massage, the masseuse tries her best with her 'massage' to arouse you so you will beg for a fuck, at *her* price, or at close to her price.

Well, he needed no persuasion, and also happens to be quite wealthy, though cheap when he can get away with it; they quickly agreed on a price for the fuck. He had stripped and was on the bed when he noticed a large, round glass-covered hole in the door; in other words, a glass window through which people walking by, whether the other girls, supervisors or customers, could see what was going on inside the room.

This upset him until she suggested they turn off the lights and do it; he agreed, believing he'd gotten off rather well.

But I challenged his assessment. After all, much of a man's pleasure from a sexual encounter is visual, and he had been denied that. Second, what if someone decided to focus a flashlight through the hole, or a flashlight and a flash camera, and clicked? The next day, the photograph of his prize, capitalist American ass would have been all over the front pages of the world's newspapers.

Obviously, this place was a victim of schizophrenic hypocrisy; the hypocritical half had installed the hole in the door so that no hanky-panky could go on; while the pragmatic, greedy, lusty other half had decided to sell sex. Were I to find myself in a room like that, I would walk out right away (unless there were absolutely no other choices for ten miles around), because I cannot even handle a normal, no-hanky-panky massage without the assurance of privacy: I need to be sure that what is going on in the massage room is strictly between me and the masseuse, and no one else's business.

Catfighting Masseuses

In Asia, you may sometimes have to deal with territorial conflicts: when one masseuse decides you are 'hers', and all others accept—at which point, changing masseuses can result in high drama. So be warned of the risks—and then choose to enjoy the proceedings, if that's your preference.

In a certain massage establishment in Cambodia, I once had to choose between two cat-fighting masseuses, with the object of the fight being me. It happened thus. Early in my visits to this place, I discovered an absolutely fantastic masseuse, Anna, who was so far superior to the local average that I asked for her on my subsequent visits.

In time, the other masseuses considered me to be hers and hers only. She did not allow me to play with her hair or touch her, nor did she kiss me at my request—the kind of thing that I am impelled to ask for when I start feeling affectionate towards a masseuse. I accepted her refusals with grace, because even without any of these extras, her massage was sublime, a gift, a huge bargain when compared to its price.

For six months, I belonged entirely to Anna. Then, when Anna went to her hometown on leave, I was forced to try Belinda, who I discovered to be equally good and a bit more playful besides, allowing me to play with her glorious long hair, among other things. I now became addicted to Belinda, and when Anna returned, Belinda rubbed it into her that she had won me, and that I was now hers. Thereafter, every time Anna looked at me, I could see in her eyes the hurt and anger of betrayal.

For an entire year thereafter, I was assigned exclusively to Belinda. However, showing up once when Belinda was busy, and being desperately in need of a massage, I asked for Anna. Anna not only gave me a fantastic massage, but while she was massaging my head, she rubbed her pussy against my head, pretending it was accidental. Well, she did indeed have her back against the wall, but neither of us was fooled, for she did this repeatedly. So, even as she continued massaging me, I, aroused, reached inside the elastic waistband of her stretch-pants and inserted my fingers into her pussy and diddled it. She carried on massaging me silently for nearly seven minutes, in the same position, while I continued diddling her, still pretending that nothing had happened, while I could feel her dripping wet.

This was very exciting for me, and when I turned over, my face up, she also allowed me to play with her hair.

However, on my next visit, it was still assumed that I was Belinda's, and that my one massage with Anna had been an exception on account of Belinda being otherwise occupied. So I returned to Belinda. Anna's anger with me at this 'second betrayal' was so unforgiving that she refused to ever massage me again. And I knew that Belinda, who had now begun to massage me even more sexily and permit me liberties that were previously refused, was doing this partly because of her ongoing catfight with Anna.

Hippo Massage

Indonesia is a huge, multicultural and multi-religious country, so do not expect my general observations about Indonesian massage to apply beyond the islands of Bali and Java, which together contain over half the population of Indonesia. Because the variations in attitudes and prejudices, from across Sumatra in the north-west to Papua in the extreme east, are huge, and I have no experience whatsoever of massage other than in Java and Bali—except for one brief interlude in northern Sumatra's Batak country, in the sparsely populated island of Samosir.

Floating in the middle of one of the largest volcanic lakes in the world, this island is indeed a paradise, except in the matter of massages. For here, where the natives have been completely Christianized, the sexual open-mindedness and relaxed nature of the Javanese and Balinese are not so easily to be found.

Noticing hardly any massage places during my walks around the island, I asked the guest house to call in a masseuse to relieve a really bad back. The woman who showed up was around fifty years old and was built like a hippopotamus, and the result was only what I could describe as the hippo massage, in which my entire body and skeletal structure were rearranged, and every plea to her to reduce the pressure brought forth nothing but laughter, and just a thirty-second period of reprieve before she returned to her normal bone-crushing self. Because of her dictatorial manner, it took me some time to realize her hands were rough, the nails uncut and filled with dirt. This meant a risk of skin infection. So at this point, I rebelled and stood firm: I told her she would have to clip her nails and wash her hands with soap, and then return to the massage. Then, I proceeded to lend her my nail clipper. She yielded to my insistence, and was a little less coarse for the remainder of the massage.

Vietnamese Baby Massage

On my first visit to Saigon, a charming city with French architecture, innumerable cafes and an immense motorcycle-borne population, a couple of hotel massages in the hotels costing around $20 to $25 a night had given me the privilege of being massaged by an exceptionally beautiful young woman, possibly around twenty-two, straddling me while wearing thin white silk shorts. The shorts formed an artistic camel-toe of her cleft, with an artistry that Michelangelo would have been proud of, even though his personal preference was guys. The camel-toe and shorts left little to the imagination; to add spice to the redhot chilli of her outfit, she also wore an attractive, minimalist white blouse (the white to signal a pseudo-medical professionalism and purity, I presume). It seemed to be the standard uniform in those hotel massage joints (these were one or two-star hotels), and it was about as convincing as Tenth Avenue junkie hookers dressed in Florence Nightingale outfits. Another feature of this and most massage places in Vietnam: your room or booth has a no-hanky-panky door with a peephole, or a partially transparent glass door, or a wooden or other screen below or above through which the massager and massaged can be observed. Probably this conveys an aura of supervision, though nothing prevents the supervisor from being 'in' on the game, permitting almost anything, and taking a cut from the proceedings.

The Saigon masseuse straddled my buttocks or my silk-shorts covered penis for 30–40 minutes while she used her hands to excite—I mean, to massage—other parts of me. Whatever the brochure had claimed it to be, this massage was pure enticement: exquisite and divine, but titillating to the limit. If I were the kind of guy who would ejaculate on the excitement alone, I would have ejaculated five times in fifty minutes. But she was also shrewd enough to cease her erotic pressure just seconds before the point of no return. Again, the goal was to exercise high-quality persuasion so that I would accept an extra—a hand job or a blow job, both of which I refused, not even asking her for her rates.

This seemed to be the Saigon specialty. I visited two other massage joints, and the procedure was exactly the same: gorgeous women, exquisite titillation, and a feeling that without sex at the end of it, you might go mad.

I had a somewhat different Vietnamese massage experience at a hill resort town north of Saigon called Dalat, 4,000 feet above sea level and sometimes called the French Alps of Vietnam for its architecture, rolling green hills and blue mountains in the distance, and its lakes. Here, I decided to visit an old hotel with a 'sauna and massage' advertised as costing 100,000 dong or five dollars a massage. I never saw the sauna, and still don't know whether there really is one. I have realized that in Vietnam, signboards are meant to be decorative, and may have no direct connection with reality: a place that advertises fried rice for 20,000 dong on its door might refuse to sell fried rice, or even flied lice, for anything less than 40,000 dong.

Paying the money in advance at the ground-floor reception, I was dispatched up an elevator to meet my would-be makers—I mean my masseuses.

Given a choice of two masseuses, I chose the older, less sexy one. First, because the sexy and pretty one had long nails—which would inhibit her ability to give me a serious massage without resulting in scratches or cuts on my skin. Second, because an older, less pretty masseuse possibly had more experience and was less likely to believe that the world owed her a living just because she was young and beautiful. And I really needed someone to work on my muscles—pain relief had priority over sexual need.

Once we were in the room, she gave me a decent massage, though in fits and starts, and only after I repeatedly made it clear to her that I would not like my 'baby' massaged, but had real body pains and needed a real massage. She kept persuading me, offering the baby massage for a mere twenty-five dollars (or five times the cost of the body massage itself), but I refused.

At some point—I now fail to see what the provocation was—she lowered her short skirt to reveal a massive bush about the size of Chad. What was she trying to do? Seduce me? Get me horny because I wasn't feeling that horny today, being focused entirely on my pain? It was a massive bush, a bush of the kind that can stagger you.

Rather overwhelmed by all that hair I asked, 'Why don't you shave it?' She seemed taken aback by my suggestion, and was disappointed that her display had not led me to go in for her 'baby massage' offer. Imagine the irony: she was willing to give a hand job or a blow job to one American dong at the mind-blowing exchange rate of 500,000 Vietnamese dongs (or $25 per American dong). Still, it was a lot cheaper than taking her to a Broadway show (which *South Park* reveals to be a secret technique for getting blow jobs). Also, in showing me her bush, she had shown me a bit of her humanity—which is what you find a lot of in Vietnam: humanity, vulnerability. And which I found a lot less of in China.

INTERLUDE 2

OUT OF BODY: CONFESSIONS AND PHILOSOPHICAL EXPLORATIONS

Is there a philosophy of massage? An epistemology, an ontology, a hermeneutics, an apologetics? Whatever the answer, this section attempts to get a couple of balls rolling.

WHILE MY GUITAR GENTLY WEEPS

There are two kinds of sins: sins of commission and sins of emission. I have erections, of course, half the time during my massages. I might be slightly embarrassed by them, but I know I can't help them, and any masseuse must know that it's an occupational hazard (or perk, if she is to see the positive side, like Mae West, who famously said, 'Is that a gun in your pocket, or are you just glad to see me?'). For some men are hornier than others, and if you can't politely ignore it, at least try not to get too steamed up about it.

But unintended sudden emissions, though nearly always occurring beneath a towel and unknown to the masseuse, seem like an incursion into the realm of illegality and trouble, especially in America. Because the unwritten and unspoken understanding seems to be: This is a therapeutic massage for pain relief, so you ought *not* to be getting any kind of sexual satisfaction. *Achtung! Eeet ees forbidden!*

But in real life, the boundaries between massage and sexual excitement are porous. How can you receive warm and intimate touches from a sweet and gentle woman without getting a bit aroused—unless you're dead down there? For me, my whole body is a sexual instrument—about the only non-erogenous parts being my knees, elbows, hair and fingernails.

Nipples and their surrounding areas, buttocks, thighs (back, front and inner), and lower abdomen, and sometimes even the flanks of my trunk, are highly erogenous—and yet, with the exception of nipples, flanks and lower abdomen, these are also the areas with the most muscular tension, the greatest in need of massage, along with my upper back and shoulders. Whereas the hands and forearms, along with the entire chest and armpits—all important areas requiring massage—are only moderately erogenous.

For years, therefore, when I was in the States, I would sometimes have an unintended emission and keep it under my hat—metaphorically speaking. It happened with Julia (sorry, Julia), with Janet (of course she had to notice, as she provided no towel, but she said nothing), and most anxiously, with my best American masseuse, Lisa. Keeping silent, I would feel a bit embarrassed. Not because my body was behaving naturally and healthily, as it should, but because I feared Lisa's later discovery of something sticky or coagulated on her sheets and towels, and the consequent banning of me (cut off in the blossoming of my sin, I think, with melodramatic exaggeration)—for she was such a fabulously good masseuse, so head and shoulders above every other masseuse for a hundred miles, that I feared the ban like I feared death.

One day, however, I thought the secret was out. Using a sheet instead of the usual towel, she had, this day, let her fingers stray on both sides of my left-leaning, 75 per cent erect penis, touching it twice, and ten seconds after she had left the scene, possibly to fetch a towel, I quickly cupped the glans in my hand and contained the spray within my palm. Within seconds she returned to the room, and noticing some disturbance, asked me, 'Everything all right?' 'Yes,' I replied, desperately trying to wipe my hands off on the sheet that I was lying on, and not having the heart to tell the truth, which was: *Heck, baby, you are all I have! It's easier to find a new lover than a good massage therapist. How can I possibly tell you what really happened, and risk losing you?* But the mystery remained: Did she know that this happened sometimes? Was she being secretly mischievous with her seemingly innocent question? After all, she was a natural, unperturbed, not uttering a meaningless 'sorry' after having twice brushed my soft-skinned but not-soft pee pee.

Barely two days later, I was back on her massage table, and perversely, my dick got hard at the mere thought of what had happened the last time, how narrow my escape had been, and I was full of anticipation and nervousness about how this naughty thing of mine was going to behave today.

And with me being already aroused by my *thought*, it happened again. This time I spurted into a towel, and seconds later, gosh, she just lifted the towel and took it away, leaving me exposed but saying nothing. *Gosh, Lisa, say something! Do you know?* I could not think of any explanation for her silence except her intrinsic kindness and charity. So later, I gifted her an autographed copy of my novel, and she hugged me for it.

For years, I suffered this conflict in silence (who knows how much business the resulting tension gave to massage therapists), often engaging in furious mental arithmetic to distract myself (and in the process, losing some of the relaxation I had come for in the first place). Finally, one day, I plucked up the courage to ask an American massage therapist I had gotten comfortable with: 'What if you have a male customer who ejaculates on the table during the massage, and you discover it later?'

'I would simply take it as something else that someone leaves on my table, like breast milk, or menstrual blood,' she replied. 'Most of the time, I wouldn't notice. But if I did, it would be okay for me if he didn't bring it up, and I didn't bring it up.'

God, what a noble and lofty woman, such wisdom and understanding there! How I wish I had heard these very words many years back. How much agony and anxiety and self-criticism it might have saved me. But now, thinking even more radically, I think perhaps the man doesn't merely need to be tolerated, he actually *needs*, or would at least be better off with, acceptance and understanding from the woman that what has happened is okay by her—for, when she is silent, he is unsure if he has it. Or if he needs forgiveness from her, in addition to his own forgiveness, does he have that?

These pleasant and comforting episodes, with Lisa and the masseuse who articulated her enlightened position, came much later. Many years earlier, a New Orleans masseuse had chased after me on the street just to hurl the accusation, 'You ejaculated!' And earlier, another masseuse had refused to massage me further because she observed a certain fluid emission. And I thought, 'So I've emigrated from a country (India) with thought control to a country with emission control? But I believe in the constitutional right to freedom of emission, and the right to the privacy of my emissions. I object to the policing of my emissions, which are as involuntary as breathing, and dependent on the complex and individualistic architecture of my brain cells—which not even thirty psychoanalysts working for thirty years will quite be able to unravel. It's not as if I turn around and shoot off into the masseuse's face and open mouth; mostly, I try to prevent it by distracting myself, but if the urge is unstoppable, I do it with the utmost care to avoid discovery or embarrassment, and yet, I cannot always expect that my trail-covering measures will be foolproof.'

Therefore, for readers in similar conundrums, I have crafted a few other post-emission-discovery responses. To a Lomilomi masseuse (Lomilomi is a traditional Hawaiian massage with music, dancing, flowing moves, and not enough massage): 'Well, I suppose I just produced a few Hawaiian mini-kids. Say hi to them, will you? Need some lomilomi juice?' Or the simpler: 'It ain't my fault, honest, I am a nice guy, but I have never been able to train my dick to think pure thoughts.'

Or a longer, more serious and philosophical explanation (take a deep breath): 'This emission is a purely physical and automatic response like a knee jerk or a sneeze, a conditional reflex, spasmodic and involuntary. The pleasure I get from a massage is from the foreplay, so to speak, that has preceded the emission—the expectation, the sensual quality of the touch, the rhythmic movements. Emission is merely a release from tension, an anti-climax rather than a climax. The only time I actually get some pleasure from emission itself is when I am making love to a woman who is exciting, who has raised the pitch of my body with a lot of foreplay, visual arousal, or emotional excitement. For women, or for other men, it may be different. It's true that the body is slightly more relaxed after the emission, making the therapeutic work of massage easier. But relaxing the customer or patient is after all the purpose of the massage. Without it a massage has failed in its primary goal, and the customer should be let off without being charged. Indeed in many cases, thanks to a bad attitude or sheer incompetence, I have left a massage more stressed and in greater pain than I was when I started.' Amen, amen.

Asian and eastern European masseuses tend to be far more relaxed about emissions, smiling gently and acceptingly at you and shushing away your embarrassed apologies. They are happy to have helped, and they feel compassion for your tense state.

One more thing: Just because I am a man, it doesn't mean I always want stimulation or ejaculation, or that it is men's preferred form of pleasure. Supposing I have an appointment with a sensual and much desired lover immediately after the massage? Unless I am young and bursting with sperm, my performance is endangered by what has happened. My mojo has been stolen, my cup has prematurely run over, and it may even cause a rift with the lover who might say, 'What happened to you today? You are always raring to go!' and might not believe my weak explanation: 'It was an accident, honey. The masseuse touched an erogenous zone repeatedly and all of a sudden, I lost control.'

Yet, accidents happen, so who are we—or anyone else—to question divine intention? The point is, that in the United States, 98 per cent of all my massages had an overwhelming motive: to relieve sore muscles, stress and an unbalanced body, and because I enjoy massage in its entirety, not because I wanted sex. If I had primarily desired sex, I would have chosen a different establishment. So honour this desire of mine, and give me the best massage you can, and let not the thought of sex cross your mind. Do not prejudge me, or even post-judge me. And whether I desire you or not—and as a weak and easily aroused human being, I might briefly desire you—I will honour and maybe even worship you for having given me a caring, compassionate, healing and superb massage. That's all you ask for—or should—right?

THE ZEN OF BALLS AND MASCULINE MAINTENANCE

We've spoken at length about women and penises—a vast subject, one must admit, deserving not just a chair (or a couch, as Sigmund Freud, the founder of penis envy, might have preferred)—yes, not just a Supreme Court bench, a casting couch, or Chair of Lingam Studies, but an entire university dedicated to research on the subject, and at least a few different versions of *Lingam Monologues* running on Broadway. But how about balls, the humbler and oft-neglected younger brothers of penises?

The good news is that many women and masseuses *do* have a soft corner for balls—a feeling warmly reciprocated by the balls themselves. Indeed, balls attract women, their magnetism operating on multiple fronts: a playful one, which may have something to do with their roundness, their vulnerability and the pivotal role that balls play in the continuation of the species—they are the fathers of the human race at the same time that they are its babies (in the Thai and Cambodian languages, the word for balls, *kai hum* or *pong khado* respectively, translate literally as 'eggs of the penis' or 'eggs of the banana'—banana being Thai slang for penis). A win–win scenario. Besides which women adore soft teddy bears, as they adore cute puppies, and it certainly helps that there are two of them, though not often identical. (One-balled Adolf Hitler would have been laughed out of any massage spa outside the Third Reich, and even the most loyal Nazi masseuse probably would have been guilty of quite a few suspicious coughs while she massaged Der Führer's pelvic *lebensraum*.) So give a woman a chance and no guilt at all, no repercussions, no legal Sword of Damocles and no kiss-and-tell, and she will play with your balls almost forever, sometimes in indirect ways—like the Jakarta masseuse who mischievously rested her bottle of oil on my balls and partly against the edge of my anus. Perhaps because balls don't have the 'forbidden fruit' or other dangerous connotations that the penis has, whereas the penis can perform some cute tricks, including sending tiny white missiles into outer space or in the direction of a salivating ovum. Besides which, a particular penis may be dirty or unwashed for months, and it could conceivably spray fluids of unknown vintage at you! Such unattractive attributes make the dick fraught with many more grave consequences than balls. Also, everyone from your mother to your elder sister has told you to be careful around men's dicks, that they are the source of most of the world's known problems (and a fair portion of the world's yet to be discovered problems). But no mother warns her daughter against balls which, after all, just lie there helplessly, doing nothing at all; they are sitting ducks, so to speak—or duck's eggs, if the Thais were commissioned to enliven the English language.

Now I don't and cannot claim to be—and will fight to the death any imputation that I might be—the world's pre-eminent authority on balls. I haven't researched them at great length, for one thing, and to be quite honest, I must confess that I haven't studied a single other pair except mine, possibly because I am not a woman, and other men's balls just bore me to death. One of the greatest annoyances for me about most erotic movies—especially the badly made ones, which I used to watch at one time, but don't any more, preferring to enact my own mild episodes whenever possible—is that depending on the kinkiness, lack of imagination, or possible homosexual leanings of the director or the cameraman, or their desire to please a possible female audience, I might be forced to watch other men's balls, sometimes in extreme close-ups, and for far too long—time I could have spent better reading *Finnegan's Wake*, *Gravity's Rainbow* or *The Music of the Spheres*. I can't speak for my fellow males—many of whom are obsessed with ball games and ball game expressions such as 'in the ball park'—but, speaking for myself, and only for myself, I emphasize that what gently touching my balls does is to arouse me, and make my dick hard and start leaking seminal fluid, perhaps one drop every ninety seconds, which of course, if noticed, might seem like a magical discovery for the masseuses, so they don't stop; it is like they have finally figured out how to operate the safety remote control and, without actually soiling their hands with the forbidden dick, have made it dance to their tune.

On the other hand, some women simply don't understand the Zen of balls, let alone of masculine maintenance. As was the case with Pattaya masseuse 'Noo No. 8', as she described herself—she simply didn't get it.

You see, ladies—or even if you don't see, and even if you are legally, morally and politically blinded on this subject, you better understand this—men's balls are a 'no speeding' zone. Just as a neighbourhood with a large number of little children will sport 'slow, children' signs on their roads, so too similar signs, prominent and unambiguous, need to be placed at about a distance of six inches in every direction from the balls: 'Slow, balls. Maximum speed: 1 mph.'

But poor Noo didn't understand that. Compassionate, eager, even horny (I say this is vehemently not true of the average Indian or Cambodian woman, but absolutely is of Thailand and Indonesia: that an extremely strong genetic propensity for survival has endowed their women with more than average horniness per capita; thus, Thai women make up in lust what they may lack, say, in their aptitude for quantum physics or for existential theory), she had of her own accord removed the towel I had draped around my waist (and the fragile 'modesty' that it covered) and had spread my legs from behind while massaging the back of my thighs.

Now that I turned over, she had my full frontal view spread out before her, and she probably was even more aroused than I. Which is when her hands, like a speeding locomotive on a slippery track, zoomed towards my groin again and again, bringing forth from me a partly self-defensive 'Ouch!', especially when the greedy and slippery fingers bumped into my balls at way above the speed limit. An instinct for self-preservation had already made me physically transport my member from the side she was working on, forcing it to lean left or right in the opposite direction, regardless of its inherent inclination of the moment. But balls are not so pliable, not so easy to cart around; they don't come with wheels. So here she was, giving me a pretty good massage, but the threat to the family jewels had me up in arms (or should I say, up in legs?). My whole system was on high alert, the anti-ballistic missiles were seconds from launch, because the High Command (yes, their Majesties, my Balls, which ruled my person, being the Reproducing Agents of the Species) had to be saved, and lesser body parts had been authorized to plan and execute suicide missions if necessary.

In any case, many of her strokes, though reluctantly avoiding my balls after I had delivered a firm warning that any further incursions would be repelled with disproportionate and overwhelming force, were pushing large quantities of oil deep into my groin. So much so that, in spite of the shower which she aided me with, raunchily groping my dick while pretending to help me, and again later when I was changing (whew! I had thought that groping was an exclusively male failing, but obviously I had never been to a ladies night at a disco or met Noo No. 8 before this), I went home and, idly feeling my groin, suddenly had the impression that I had struck oil, and in quantities that made the Persian Gulf seem rather arid.

Now let me give you another story of one more masseuse who had a special affection for balls.

In Phnom Penh, Cambodia, I was in a joint with A-class masseuses and few inhibitions about male anatomy—rare qualities in Cambodia, which suffers from a rather milder form of India's moral split personality: social pressure for a public pretence of virtue and sexual conservatism from its women. My usual, experienced masseuse being busy, I nervously tried the younger girl, Linda, perhaps twenty-one, who I assumed would disappoint, being inexperienced and unacquainted with my peculiar needs and dislikes. But, after I explained to her that my back, especially my upper and lower back, needed particular attention, she proceeded to give me one of the best lower back massages I have ever had.

So good was she that, sooner rather than later, something would happen, I anticipated, especially now that her hands were roaming freely from my inner thighs to my balls and up to caress my lower buttocks. All this with the smooth, silky hands of a lovely masseuse. And this dreaded but nevertheless exciting something happened, and when it did, it had that way of spraying into a lower corner of my thigh and the towel to evade discovery. Fearing a discovery in any case, I immediately distracted her by asking her to start re-massaging my shoulder. Having diverted her, I mentally assessed the damage: so arousing had her touches been that every sperm that was remotely in attendance, and even a few that were legally off on their lunch break, was given the bum's rush and catapulted out within seconds. I was so completely drained it felt as if it could take a long, long time before my balls would ever feel full again.

When I turned over, my eyes and hers met, and she smiled, and this happened around ten times in the next forty-five minutes of this two-hour massage, and somehow I noticed a greater intimacy in the way we were now looking at each other; it is as if in the episode of the balls, we had shared something intimate, a partial embrace of souls, and she knew it, and felt closer to me.

Pleased at this connection, I returned a few days later, and this time she didn't need a request from me, nor did she ask permission: it was as if her hands were a soft, soft shoe brush, the oil shoe polish, and she giving me a gentle but perfect shoe shine—on the back of my balls and buttocks—in preparation for the grand inspection by a visiting general or president. How dedicated and unrestrained. Once again, within a few minutes, a few million helpless wrigglers shot off into the spaces between the interstices of my towel.

Ah, relief. Ah, ecstasy. And gratitude from me, for her kindness. This is why, I remind myself, I should not be so closed-minded. I should be open to trying new masseuses—because sometimes, trying a new masseuse is like trying a new lover. If it turns out nicely, the ecstasy and gratitude of the first time is in a special class of its own, and will always, always be superior to a tenth night with Angelina Jolie or Megan Fox.

There's another reason why masseuses are always more liberal with your rear (which is the preferred access point to the balls) than they are with the corresponding parts in front: because they are getting an eyeful, but without them being caught in the act. Your eyes are not staring them down and theirs are free to roam anywhere without risk of discovery, without having to pretend to be uninterested or casual. Besides, lying face down, you are immobile, unable to suddenly turn around and attack, and, in effect, harmless—and this harmlessness makes them feel more comfortable and more daring.

More power to them.

Before I end, let me mention another masseuse whose ingenuity was a tribute to women's creativity. She, being a mother of two in a conservative country, was totally in charge; I gave her general directions, but was passive on the table. Her technique was to place the towel over my belly and legs in a way that it arched away from her, thus exposing around one-fifth of my pubis and groin (the side she was working on), a side view of my balls, and the entirety of my inner thigh, but absolutely none of the well-sequestered penis—so that she could never, ever be accused of decadence, neither in this life or the next. And I was grateful for her thoughtfulness, because the pubis and the groin are important, but often neglected by the prudish. Massaging my thighs starting from above my groin, she made it a point to gently bump against the side of my balls during each up and down motion. I hope her contribution to the universe of balls is recognized with a honorary Ph.D from Ball State University (Indiana).

PART IV

MASSAGE INDIAN-STYLE: THINK TWICE BEFORE SHAKING HANDS

In India, the land of my birth and the birthplace of Ayurvedic massage, tantric sex and Rajneesh (who preached sexual liberation to Germans and Swedes), and of course the holy *Kamasutra*, globalization and liberalization have recently changed the face of the metropolis, as Thai masseuses are imported to work in exclusive spas and five-star hotels, and lingam massage is offered in provocatively worded personals in 'free ad' magazines, even in conservative Chennai. But when I began hunting for Indian massage joints in the mid-nineties and the early noughties on my trips to India from the US, the situation was discouraging, varying from the boringly legal, unpleasant and dangerously incompetent to the scarily illegal and nutty. The social critique in this section, though describing mainly that period, is retained partly for its authenticity, comic value, description of the milieu and sociological observations—for its being a snapshot of a moment in time—but also because many of the repressive conditions are still true for the un-liberated and economically less privileged majority of Indians, whose healthy natural impulses are still repressed by a cautious, guarded society.

14

THE HANDSHAKE OR THE MILKING OF THE INDIAN MALE

Despite appearances, you will discover that India, or at least the world of Indian massage parlours, the ones that have been mushrooming recently in cities like Bangalore, is a very Westernized place, because instead of the traditional Indian namaste, or greeting with folded hands, they will offer, on their unofficial menu, a handshake.

Yes, you heard right: a *handshake*. Those of you who think, 'Well, what's so unusual or bizarre about a handshake, and why mention it on a menu—let alone on an *unofficial* menu'—let me explain with an imaginary, but not improbable, dialogue, partly in Indian English.

At this Bangalore massage joint called Satisfaction Spa, disguised as a beauty parlour (there are a few barber's chairs in the mainly for show entrance hall, but not the forest of hair on the floor and the vaguely cloying smell of cheap talcum powder that you find in the average Indian barbershop), I enter a little massage cubicle in the rear section of the establishment, following a dusky south Indian girl in a sari and coconut-oiled long hair, some jasmine flowers pinned to a single braid. Her laughing, wily eyes are peering at me with curiosity.

'Do you want a handshake?' the girl (she's possibly around twenty-three, but to describe her as a woman would probably be to insult her—she's so slim and girl-like) asks, once I am as comfortable as I can be on a somewhat precarious and narrow massage table, one of its legs a bit shorter than the other three.

'Of course, yes! I've no objection to shaking your hand,' I reply, not wishing to be unfriendly on the first encounter.

'I mean, a shake *with* my hands.' Her face seems nervous, while her smile broadens.

'A milk shake that you'll make with your hands?' I ask, looking flustered.

'*Your* milk, sir.' More serious, almost demure.

'Excuse me, but you must have gotten my sex wrong. The last I checked, and that was just a few minutes back, I was a man. So sorry, but I don't think you can rely on me for milk production.'

'No, sir, I shake your *little* hand. The little, itty-bitty hand between your legs. With my big hand.'

'Oh, you mean my *short* hand!' The natives do indeed have quaint customs, I must say, even though I am a 101 per cent native myself, reinvented in Noo Yawk, Yemerica, no less. 'But why, my dear, could you possibly want to shake that slippery little hand of mine?'

'For the milk, sir. I mean, for the milk from your pen-neese.'

'Milk? Either you are shockingly innocent, or udderly misinformed. The stuff that spurts out of the full-mast pen-neese, as you call it, is not milk, you know. The milk of human kindness, perhaps, but not milk that is fit for consumption by persons under the age of eighteen.'

'I mean, the water, sir. '

'I don't own an organ, madam, even though I once owned a mouth organ, and am fond of organ music and of organic food when it doesn't taste like sawdust; but *if* I did own an organ, I wouldn't place too much reliance on it for water.'

'I mean your *male* organ, sir.'

'As opposed to my female organ? Anyway, my male organ. Oh, I get it. So you're going to shake it for milk or water?'

'Yes, sir. That's the handshake. That will be 400 rupees extra.'

'What?! Get outta here! I have never heard of anyone charging for a handshake! It sounds rather unfriendly, what?!'

'No, sir, *you* get outta here. Our policy is: no milk, no honey.'

End of imaginary dialogue, which is a composite from many different snatches of real dialogue, and of actions and policies that are unspoken. Though it makes me wonder: why do these people have to torture themselves with such strained euphemisms for penis when the Indian vocabulary contains a majestic equivalent: lingam?

Perhaps this dialogue is a demonstration of mere technical quibbling, mere spoilt-child banter, the superciliousness of the Indian privileged bourgeois classes towards their fellow Indians from more repressed backgrounds who must speak in tortured euphemistic language while working at these joints. But the bourgeois customers little realize that they are the greater bakras (and the bakras include me, for when I have been in India longer than two or three weeks, there is no bakra in the world who looks as meek and distressed as I do), with that desperate look on their sad faces that betray that they have no option but to subject themselves to any degrading humiliation the girls have to offer, so long as it is some form of recognition that they are human, with organs, with organs that have needs, with male organs that have special needs, one of which consists of being milked or hand-shaken at least once in a month, if not twice a week weakly (forget the daily milking, that is only for the far luckier cows of India, whose sacred right of teat-illation is enshrined in the sacred Indian constitution). (So desperate are we that if *hand*shakes were not available, we would even consent to leg shakes or toe shakes.)

Bakras they indeed are, most Indian massage customers, for the girls grimly order them to wear shorts, or to keep their underwear on. What's worse (and this happened to me once at an Ayurvedic joint of the strictly non-milking breed), they are sometimes asked to wear funny little, tightly tied *kachchas*, *kashtis* or *langotis*—elongated loincloths, Vedic Xtra-large fat boy G-strings *pour homme*—sometimes by stern male masseurs (who have been trained to affect the stern expressions of headmasters scolding dirty little boys), and sometimes by masseuses. Who knows how many smelly behinds these loincloths have previously dug deeply into in the process, absorbing into their molecular or atomic innards their noxious body effluents? But the Indian bakras meekly obey; indeed they allow themselves to be subjected to this humiliation, this charade, this infantilization, this shrinking of their manhood or humanity, because they desperately yearn to be touched by a woman or a man (yes, even a man will do sometimes), and also to be milked, if they are lucky enough to be in the right place with a willing milkmaid.

I admit that I, too, on a few desperate occasions, have submitted to the fascist knotting up, as when I agreed to let his august eminence, my sri sri buttocks, and other pelvic appendages, be tightly knotted and bundled up within a kaccha or mini-loincloth at an Ayurvedic joint in nineteenth-century Mangalore (yes, which in the twenty-first century is still suffocated by a two-century-old morality, and where women were recently beaten for drinking in pubs). I yielded, because it would have been impossible to argue with the humourless Keralite masseur, whose intelligence and exposure to Euro-American ideas of born clothes-free nudist liberation were sorely limited. However, at the Bangalore place I had discovered in 2004—which had a Manipuri masseuse who knew me as a regular customer, and where they had suddenly and unilaterally introduced these paper G-strings in 2006, apparently in response to a recent police instruction, threat or raid—I argued with the masseuse. I told her it was a childish requirement, reducing me to the status of a small boy; it was like having a shower with a raincoat on, and that I didn't like the fake puritanical gesture in this obviously puritan-defying establishment.

I conclusively asserted that I wasn't going to wear that pansy little male panty even if she paid me to do it. And I won my case, for she knew I had lived abroad and travelled widely, and that I was not going to stand for such nonsense. As for her, personally, it didn't matter one bit—she was a Manipuri, from a north-east Indian tribal culture that is much more comfortable with the body, that has significantly more affinity with Thai and Vietnamese culture than with Indian. Besides which, she had seen everything that could possibly be seen (not so difficult, because the human species comes in basically two models, with only minor variations of size and elasticity), and it was all natural—as natural as shaking hands, or in this case, shaking *little* hands, which she did with a song in her heart if not on her lips. This is one of the great virtues of the girls who come from the north-eastern hilly regions of India, as indeed of most of neighbouring Southeast Asia. They are not surprised or threatened—let alone shocked or traumatized—by the human anatomy, and have a relaxed, cheerful and realistic attitude towards life. And they must have laughed at the hypocrisy of ordering their shrunken male customers to wear silly-looking, ill-fitting paper shorts, only to slip them down later in the course of the massage to execute their professional, wholesome, and wholly holy therapeutic handshake.

While 98 per cent of India (that is, except the north-east) is choked by the langoti or loincloth-cum-Vedic-G-string of repression, such micro-sartorial oppression is not the fate of the privileged customer who frequents the world of the high-class massage parlours and five-star masseuses of India. Such masseuses flourish in premier hotels and certain exclusive spas with hedonistic auras that have sprung up in the metropolitan centres and the playgrounds of the super-rich. They are often brought in from Thailand, north-eastern India, or countries or states where sex is not a taboo, or, in fact, is considered a healthy and even sacred expression of one's humanity, like a three-Martini lunch, a languorous hot bath, a visit to the temple or a postprandial walk. In these enclaves of privilege, the customers pay sixty to ninety dollars for an hour, or exactly the same as they would pay in New York (but five times as much if you factor in India's far lower cost of living); in return, they are permitted to lie in their glorious nudity under luxurious Turkish towels, towels which are manipulated by the masseuse, and sometimes—according to my upscale informant, the son of a senior police officer—simply lifted away for a bit of necessary and compassionate oxygenation of the pitifully suffocated areas, whereupon a smidgeon of exhibitionism on the part of the customer does not immediately evoke a stern rebuke or a tightening of the screw—I mean, of the langoti, kashti or such other anti-penile weapon, which may also double up as a weapon of arse destruction, division or obstruction. Indeed, there is no kashti permitted within a mile of these joints, which follow a strict 'leave your kashti at the door' policy. It is all spotless towels and clean white bed sheets. Why this disparity, this apparent discrimination? Because the customers hail from the master class (all heil!), being the sort of worthies and eminences who holiday in London and Greece and the Riviera if not *being* from there, or are wealthy and pampered tourists like the author and Indophile Paul Theroux, who could probably pay as much as Governor Eliot Spitzer did for a night with his high-class fillies de joie and not think twice about it. So it is assumed they've seen it all, and at this steep price will not tolerate being talked down to and have their 'little brothers' shrunk in size and status.

Sadly, it's always been a double world in India, a world of double, triple or quadruple standards of morality and justice, of multiple societies living side by side, breathing the same air of sixty-plus years of freedom from British rule, with the loot now being fairly divided between the political and financial master classes.

15

GENTS FINGERS: A DISSECTION OF INDIAN MASSAGE

Until the beginning of the millennium, nearly all of my massages in India consisted of reluctantly and apprehensively surrendering my near-naked body to men I had never before met in my entire life, men I couldn't imagine having a long conversation with because we had so few interests in common, and so few linguistic bridges. Things have indeed changed dramatically in the last few years in the cities, but India is a country in which a multitude of eras or centuries coexist simultaneously—medieval and lower-caste-burning Bihar coexisting with wife-swapping rings in Bombay and Bangalore; even in Bombay, the moral attitudes and living standards of those in posh, sea-viewing, multi-million-dollar apartments of Bandra or Andheri being a universe apart from the middle-class Navi Mumbai—or greater Bombay connected to the main city by a buzzing network of trains—which is again worlds apart from the chawls and slums of Mahim or Khar. So please forgive me if my early experiences of Indian massage often bristle with irritation, fear, annoyance, frustration and unforgivable ill-humour—yet they also overflow with sympathy for the many poor people who are needlessly victimized in the country of my birth and the country that I love. To sanitize my emotion and the language of the original with the wisdom of afterthought would have violated its authenticity. I trust the original emotion, and believe in the importance of the writer giving it to the reader naked, unedited, un-bowdlerized and un-purified by Protestant stuck-upness or politically correct sterilization. So here goes.

Scene: Bangalore, December 1997. In Bangalore, where you can find high-speed Internet access and beer pubs in every second block, and bountiful quantities of beautiful babes who fill their overflowing blouses and jeans with their joie de vivre (and also with their delectable tits and asses), and which is sometimes called a poor man's paradise, don't expect a paradise for the poor man's tool, and don't expect to easily get a massage from a woman. For a massage parlour you may need to take a four-hour flight to Bangkok, nothing less, and there you can also get, in addition to your massage, your fill of roast duck, dancing shrimp, naked shrimp, totally naked shrimp, stripper shrimp and raw papaya salad. Whereas in India, whose literature, language, culture and religions have deeply influenced many Asian countries, it would be easier for a man to get massaged by a cow than by a woman. And should you wish to innovate and start a religion based on cow massage and call it Moossage, with the slogan 'The Message Is Moossage', you would not only succeed, you would become fabulously wealthy, and your cool Sri Sri Cowashram would soon overflow with milk and imported goris or white honeys. But just don't ever expect a massage from a woman.

What you *may* have in Bangalore is a distant, illegitimate and leprous cousin of the real thing, a massage by a man who gives you the creeps, a barely trained man who will pour what feels like a bucket of coconut oil onto every part of you, and then slide his sweaty and rough hands up and down your body at supersonic speed while he rocks on the balls of his feet for leverage and uses your bones (and sometimes your balls) as speed bumps and turn signals (since these massage rooms are usually semi-dark, his hands have to rely on the braille system to read traffic signals, which are inconsistent and unreliable due to the varying sizes and proportions of body parts in every man). At the end of this 'massage', you will find yourself with an extremely oily body that will take two hours to de-oil and detoxify, possibly by repeatedly using a combination of ash, dried coconut husk and Lux beauty soap, and when this is over and the grease and smell finally off you, you may realize that you are left with bones that hurt and muscles that have merely been given a superficial shine (the masseur having made the same moves as he would were he giving you a shoe shine, except that in this case the shoe happens to be your poor self).

Once, in the mid-1990s, when I was a long-time guest at a tea estate located at around six thousand feet above sea level in a cloud-kissed section of the Nilgiris in south India, and in desperate body pain, I reluctantly surrendered to a massage from an Indian labourer who had worked in the bungalows of tea-estate owners. I found his hands inching towards my bottom and to the crevice in my bottom, without my asking for it. It was somewhat roughly erotic, his hands being anything but the smooth female hands that turn me on, but disturbing too, and I wondered whether this was normal, whether he did it with his tea-planter masters, or whether my request that he do it in my bedroom and not in the open, because I am self-conscious about being massaged where others can see me, was taken by him as a cue that I wanted a somewhat more intimate massage. And because of the language gap, I could do nothing; it was pointless anyway!

Anyway, he did my back and my arms (not my front, I didn't allow him, as I was not ready for any more surprises), with medium pressure, for about twenty-five minutes. After that, I had a shower. And then I discovered, walking through the hills later in the afternoon, that I was weaker; I had been walking around quite energetically with just a little back ache for the last few days, but I could now barely walk a tenth of that distance. I felt almost out of sorts, as if I had been taken apart and then screwed back together without the body parts matching. What's the message? That massage loosens your muscles and weakens you, and like masturbation according to certain Indian texts, causes a leakage and loss of the strength and toughness and life spirit you have accumulated? Or, is it that an *unbalanced* massage—which this certainly was, as I had asked him not to massage my front—weakens you? I have no answer, though I have often limped home after an incomplete massage (one leg, or one side of the body done, after which I was told my time was up), so I think these questions deserve far more and well-funded research for the benefit of mankind, massage being no longer the privilege or kinky hobby of the well-heeled, aristocratic or royal few, but a major part of the preventive health system in many countries.

Scene: Mangalore, April 1999. From Bangalore I now move my tale of men-on-men massage to coconut-palmed Mangalore, my multi-ethnic and multilingual hometown, and a poor man's gourmet paradise in the south-west of India. The setting is a hotel named Mohan Mahal, just two minutes from the town's centre, and behind which there once existed a forest-dense coconut plantation, but has now been levelled and replaced with an ugly concrete marriage hall. After receiving a simply atrocious massage from a stocky, body-builder masseur at the adjoining, but not officially connected, health club, I realized why it had been so. He had caught me with my pants down, so to speak, so he could get away with a bad massage. What he had done on entering the room, and seeing me on the table with a towel draped across my middle, was to persuade me to hand him the towel and expose my naked body to his gaze. As if that was the usual procedure in this place. Once that happened, he started massaging me with long strokes rolling up my leg towards my pelvic junction, in the process lightly brushing over the side of my penis when his hands came down on their return stroke. *In his mind*, it was as if he had done me a favour, or that I had implicitly solicited and then cooperated in something illegal, and now the power balance had shifted to *him*. I say in his mind—because in such situations, no matter that I may have personally leaped ahead or sideways from the local way of thinking (in which for a stranger to have seen your private parts or bum line might be 'shame' enough to justify suicide), a sort of Gresham's Law of thought operates, and the moth-eaten thought drives out the more liberated (mine, of course).

So now, once he had established his dominance, *in his mind*, his strokes became so mechanical, so piston-like, so absurdly macho—a few hits, a few squeezes, in some absurd machine-like rhythm—that there was no therapeutic purpose to it at all, except to say: *This is my mumbo jumbo, and it's my territory, and this is what I do, okay?* I ended up with most parts feeling sore and uncared for. He had over-squeezed a few parts, while racing over important areas such as my forearms. And the hits, the slaps and the karate chops that Indian masseurs claim to be part of their technique he executed despite my protests; it was as if he wanted to exhibit his expertise in the field, display how sure he was of himself, and how contemptuous of my reservations and my unique and different body.

And I now realize that I had suffered through it because of my mute consent to his lifting my towel instead of insisting on having it drape at least my penis—which I later managed to insist on halfway through the massage.

Scene: Mysore, June 2000. Now I come to the once royal capital of Mysore, with its palaces, broad roads and the surprisingly comforting smell of horses and horse dung in the streets, where time seems to have stood still despite the arrival of the twenty-first century, where cows double as garbage disposers and traffic control officers, and thin, timid, dark-lipped girls walk the streets wearing cotton saris or long, floor-length skirts. Like Bangalore, Mysore is also sometimes called the poor man's Ooty, or the poor man's hill station. Here, I would say the massages at the Kaynes Hotel were reasonably good; also recommended are the Southern Star Hotel and the Lalith Mahal Palace Hotel, which I didn't try. But what I remember most—and I cannot place the precise location now—is an Ayurvedic massage on a table, wearing a fig-leaf langoti which is untied when you are lying on your front so they can massage your buttocks while keeping a great-germ-walling one-inch distance from your bum line all over. The massage consists of an unending mechanical repetition of long and hard strokes (the only thing missing is the metallic 'clack!'), and the masseur's defence (if they are from Kerala, they always have a defence!) of this punishing regime is: 'This is our *traditional* massage.' Maybe, but these chaps simply don't have the feeling for the real and unique human being on their table, and perhaps that's traditional too? For they are too dominated and ruled by their training, their rote, their so-called technique, the patient or customer or bakra on the table being merely the inanimate object upon which this routine is performed. And at some level, you sense that for most of these Ayurvedic masseurs, it's simply a job—they would rather have been in the Indian customs service collecting bribes, or in some Persian Gulf sheikhdom making money in some desk job—it's just that they didn't have the intelligence or the drive to make it elsewhere.

Scene: Goa, November 2004. Two days after my arrival in the overgrown beachside village of Colva in south Goa, on a sunny and pleasant afternoon, I walked into one of those ubiquitous Kerala Ayurvedic massage centres that have sprung up in the neighbouring village of Benaulim with its spectacular white-sand beaches and rhythmically flowing waves—an enclave devoted to serving sophisticated foreigners and, only grudgingly, the occasional Indian. 'Can I get a massage from a woman?' I asked the man at the front desk. At which he pointed to a sign that said 'Ladies for Ladies, Gents for Gents', and repeated the words aloud. ('Gents' is an

Indian English contraction for gentleman, usually spelt with an initial capital and applying to all males of the human species, regardless of how gentle or rough, how masculine or effeminate, and how old or young they are—yes, even a four-year-old boy with a microscopic prick is a 'gent'.)

I replied, 'I may look illiterate, but I actually can read. However, I am not comfortable with a man touching my body.'

At which a fat middle-aged female masseuse, who had been glaring at me from a seat at the reception area, screeched: *It is immoral and indecent! My brother and sister are in the police! I will tell them!*

Fortunately, not everyone thought as she did, because at an Ayurvedic massage centre a mile away, I was massaged by a woman named Mary for four hundred rupees—a placid, kind and sincere massage during which I didn't witness any explosion of immorality and indecency, either from Mary or from me. But even in 2004, in this tiny cosmopolitan enclave called Goa, this was a rare exception to the then prevailing Indian norm of 'Gents for Gents', and it turned out to be a somewhat less than relaxed massage for me, for I had been initially asked to keep my underwear on, and felt guilty for having asked to be allowed to take it off so my boxers wouldn't get oil stains.

And to think that this was Goa in 2004, a place that is famous all over the world as a haven of beauty and tolerance, of cosmopolitanism and enlightenment!

Scene: New Delhi, February 2006. Two years later I was at the country's capital for the World Book Fair. On a cold, windy and grey February day I checked into a modest south Delhi guest house, one of those numerous, nondescript guest houses halfway between the airport and Connaught Place, where the rooms are air-conditioned and aloo paratha with curd is always on the menu. Here, my body was wracking with pain, for I hadn't had a good massage for three weeks, having been travelling through India, except for those two maddening up-and-down piston-style Ayurvedic massages, rendered mechanically by morose male automatons. So I called up the Hyatt hotel, which had masseuses. However, it turned out that like Bombay's Taj Mahal hotel, they would only massage a resident guest.

So I found myself racing in a freezing autorickshaw to Lajpatnagar, to some joint the autorickshaw driver apparently knew, only to be driven round and round in that infernal three-wheeler and to discover that the place had closed. After which, returning to my hotel in disgust and defeat, I called up one of the 'home service' advertisements from the *Hindustan Times* classified columns, possibly under the heading of beauty services or 'health massage', resigned to being manhandled by a prick—I mean a male animal.

'What service do *you* want?' the man at the other end asked. It was a guy named Bob or Ron, impersonating a loaded, ambiguous voice.

'Massage, and nothing else,' I replied, earnestly and emphatically.

The guy who arrived at my hotel, and who from his height and appearance was likely a pahadi from the Uttar Pradesh or Himachal Pradesh hill regions (Bob or Ron, my foot!), was wearing long hair, dark glasses and a black leather baseball cap, and jeans so tight it probably took him about five minutes of rough persuasion to make them wriggle up his thighs. His speech alternated between English and Hindi, his sorely limited English being of a very Indian heartland kind.

He then went to the bathroom to wash, and then, to my astonishment, emerged with his pants off and only in his shirt and V-shaped briefs (the tacky cap and glasses had also, thankfully, disappeared). In consternation, I demanded that he put his pants back on pronto, which he did reluctantly, after explaining that they were tight. (Yes, poor chap, what a hindrance to blood circulation and to a good massage clothes were, and would I have objected to a masseuse taking off her clothes just to get more comfortable? Me, the bloody sexist?! No, I would have popped a bottle of virtual champagne. How unjust life is!). Sure, his pants were tighter than an ant's vagina, which is why, even with them back on his person, they were at present partly unbuttoned.

Still uncomfortable, I thought: I have called him anyway, and I need a massage so badly because my muscles are on strike; besides, I will have to pay up regardless. So I lay down and hoped for the best. He began the massage. He was pretty strong, and knew some good strokes. But he's racing through the massage like a doggie after a flung doggie toy, spending about five minutes on each major body part like the back, and the back of the legs. Then I discovered his massage was designed to be only half-an-hour long, which was half of my minimum requirement at that point. So I offered to pay a little extra in return for more time, being careful however to keep the towel on to discourage any straying of his hands, and found to my relief that he'd gotten the message.

Then I realized I had a social or environmental problem to reckon with: this poor, comically costumed bloke was not only spotted entering my room, but possibly had his DNA mapped by the omnipresent piercing and prying eyes of the Indian looking class, and he probably had to explain himself to the receptionist and the doorman, if not also the hotel dog and the hotel cat. What would the hotel desk clerk think? Would he or anyone else believe in my 'innocence', whatever that was? Maybe someone who had read my writing, and knew me to be robustly heterosexual, would not suspect me of a homosexual encounter, or would not much care in any case; but I could have no such luck in a place where the overwhelming majority didn't read English fiction, and considered homosexuality to be depraved.

It's a pity they sent a guy like that. Almost as if to shame me and to blackmail me (and here, I am thinking *their* thoughts, how amazingly quick we can be to absorb the prejudices and narrow-mindedness of our environment, letting these overtake our real and formerly liberal selves). I think: they've got the wrong guy. But at least I won't use this hotel anymore.

What a joke this incident makes of the usual moralistic and stern response: 'Of course it's gents for gents and ladies for ladies!' For, by frowning on any possibility of closeness between the opposite sexes, and by assuming that disgusting hanky-panky can be the only result of any opposite-sex contact, they are in fact not just winking at, but encouraging the flowering of a frustrated or resigned homosexuality among those who are naturally heterosexual—and paradoxically so in a country where homosexuality is absurdly, and anachronistically, a crime. Call me prejudiced, but I think you're far better off facilitating healthy heterosexual sex, even to the comically paternalistic degree that Singapore does, rather than forcing purely heterosexual but frustrated men to experiment with homosexual sex—which will only end up making them feel guilty, confused and perhaps worse. (What's worse? Search me.)

Why can we not be straight with each other? (No pun intended.)

But how can you explain to someone who doesn't understand your language (while you, bad boy, don't understand his!) that what you're interested in is a pure therapeutic massage, and nothing of a homoerotic or even erotic nature, that in fact you are close to homophobic (if apologetically so), and are only with extreme reluctance allowing another man to touch you because getting a woman to massage you in Delhi, or for that matter nearly any part of India except perhaps in the shady beauty parlours of Bombay, is as difficult as getting a date with Cindy Crawford. Especially when the very presence of the man, his peculiar appearance (a leather-and-bondage motorcycle chic bhaiyya) and his corny attempts to seduce you by leaving his pants open and almost falling off his hips, makes your face go red, yet you think of this as a bit of penance or mortification that you must suffer in silence, not for past karmic sins, but because of the pain relief your body so desperately needs.

Besides, I couldn't tell him to get out simply because I suspected he was a homosexual, could I? That was his personal space and choice, and so long as he did his job and nothing more, I could not afford to be guilty of anti-gay prejudice, which is a cruel thing, right?

It was only later that I realized that all my lofty idealism was bullshit in a sexually confused and morally messed up society, for I would have to contend with the smirks of the bellboys and the distancing of the reception manager, for whom all such idealistic argumentation was abstruse and foreign. In their view, the chap who had visited me was a fag, and a fag who flaunted it, and if he was in my room for an hour, and if I hadn't thrown him out—or even more propah, called the cops on him—I was a fag too. Oops, oops, oops!

Now, why is it so tough to get a woman to massage you in India, and why did I recoil from the man who said, 'Gents for Gents, and Ladies for Ladies', and from the very thought that not delicate, life-giving feminine fingers, but lusty, crude gents fingers would roam with impunity over my rather sensitive, nude, defenceless body? (Even though, admittedly, it could sometimes turn out the other way around—the lady could be a menacing female with sandpaper hands, and the man a gentle part-time writer with soft palms.)

Because it brought back a memory of something that had happened about several years back, in a five-star hotel. In the nineties, five-star hotels were the only place in conservative sections of south India where a man could get himself a massage in reasonably hygienic surroundings—that too, only from a male therapist. I remembered that one rascal in such a place had suddenly darkened the lights and started manipulating a certain protuberant part of my anatomy without my permission and before I could stop him. It was embarrassing, and by the time my 'No, no, stop!' had registered with him, I was angry and ashamed that I had already been handled (handballed?) against my will. And I had run away from that place and its roaming gents fingers. Soon I understood, from other almost-moves in other five-star hotels, that this was the custom, the expected gesture, the unspoken norm—built into the 'plan'.

Which is why I was right to fear men more than I feared women. Yes, men could help untie some knots, or at least loosen a few specific sore muscles if they had decent training and experience, but my entire system was cowering in fright and with distasteful anticipation of the moment when the said gent's fingers might begin their explorations of Martian terrain—whereupon the reaction would be a terrified tightening of my muscles, frustrating the very point of the massage.

Also, men by nature are often playing power games with each other. Or else, they are insecure about their own manliness or are fighting their own homophobia. In such intimate situations, undercurrents like these can ruin the tranquillity and the care needed in a massage.

So in the end, after a few weeks of tolerating epidermal starvation in India, when my muscle aches became unbearable, I would simply fly off to Southeast Asia for a break and splurge in the massage parlours of Thailand and Indonesia, sometimes having two one-hour massages daily for the first week. Tell me, why does a man have to run away from his own country, merely to be touched by a female human being, of which the country possesses approximately 500 million specimens? Surely, a country that has purged itself of other antiquated or irrational Victorian vestiges in its laws can trash its prejudice against adult women touching consenting adult men, or vice versa? These sexual barriers make us emotionally infantile, because it is as if, despite having attained maturity, society is still treating us like little children who must be told what we can and cannot do.

True, in the past three years, there have been increasing numbers of advertisements for opposite sex massage in India's metropolises, but they come at too high a price. In India, where breakfast including coffee and tea can be had for as little as forty cents, or less than half the price of an equivalent breakfast in the cheapest countries of the world, money, money and big money is what they want for kneading you. Whereas in Southeast Asia, a massage from a woman can be had for as little as two to five times the cost of a breakfast, in Bangalore, it will cost you forty times.

In Bangalore, in the one place I could find in 2002 that did a decent professional job of a massage by a female (that is, it wasn't a crude sexual massage by impatient and untrained semi-prostitutes), I would be advised to arrive in a certain general area, almost one hour of a bumpy autorickshaw ride out of the city centre, and then to make a phone call, so that one of the massage joint's spies could then pick me up, after having presumably screened me to assure themselves that I was not an undercover cop or some other kind of undesirable low-life. No, the address could not be provided; you then had to ride to the place over still bumpier roads on the pillion of the spotter's old scooter. The journey to and fro, including the screening delays, took around three hours, in addition to an hour and twenty minutes for the massage and the shower: totaling up to four wasted hours for an hour's massage.

This is why a massage by a woman is so expensive in India. Because here, the moment you utter the word 'massage', they are thinking: 'This man is weak and needy; he needs an *illegal* service, so let's exploit him and make big bucks.' If an hour's massage by a woman in a basic massage shop costs Rs 1,200 an hour, or one-third the monthly salary of an Indian clerk, and four to five times the price of a one-hour massage by a man, I am being levied a Sin Tax of over 300 per cent for having preferred a woman!

In Bangalore, between 2004 and 2006, I became friendly with a woman who ran the show at one establishment that employed four masseuses who did a fairly decent and conscientious job, though at the steep price of Rs 800 for forty-five minutes. And then one day, she confided in me that she paid Rs 75,000 a month in payoffs to various police officials, who reasoned with her that if the women were touching men, it could be viewed as possible prostitution—which in India is as close to a capital offence as one can get. So after paying the staff and the rent, she was left with a profit of about Rs 25,000 a month, which she admitted was not so bad compared to some other professions—but of course she couldn't charge Rs 300 a massage and still pay the cops.

The only remedy, as I see it, is for women's and feminist organizations to start low-cost massage clinics in which poor and unemployed women are trained in the art of massage, and men are warmly welcomed and given massages for two hundred rupees an hour. A ferocious feminist could stand guard at each such clinic, armed with a hotline to an Amazonian super-feminist who would give a telephonic tongue-lashing to any cop who dared show up to extort money.

Further, it is necessary to obliterate the shame surrounding massage. Which is why I think we should start a National University of Massage Arts, offering a short course in sex and massage education for couples before marriage. And also open hundreds of open-as-daylight massage therapy centres in all Indian cities. At least one hundred establishments in each of the five major metropolises, and twenty each in the next twenty cities, with trained therapists. To start with, let the cheaper establishments have booths with curtains and unlocked doors; only the 'good behaviour' of the customer will entitle them to progress to the ones with locked doors (all said and done, I admit I don't want someone bursting in on me while I am having a massage, and a semi-intimate part of me is being touched—the very risk of that would make me—I mean my whole body—shrink). Sure, there are going to be a few abuses, but the present set-up with its increased risks of HIV and blackmail, is far, far worse. Such a programme will increase employment opportunities for underpaid and underemployed women at many times the minimum wage, besides causing a huge spike in the happiness quotient of Indian manhood and womanhood.

16

INDIAN MASSAGE: ZOOMING INTO MODERNITY

The recent sexual revolution among the upper-middle and middle-middle classes has made it possible today to get a masseuse in India, though still at prohibitively expensive prices—around Rs 1,250 and up (house calls are double and higher, going up to between Rs 7,500 and Rs 10,000 for Russian girls), compared to a massage by a male, which could be as cheap as Rs 250 an hour. This in a country where a superb multi-course south Indian vegetarian meal can still be had for Rs 50 or less! Ah, a land where you can eat away your sexual frustrations.

But back in September 2004, things were different. I was in Bangalore, where the upper-class and fashionable college women are sexy, frisky and impossible to miss, and yet, the pleasure they offer is mainly a visual feast, without touch or personal contact, and this can be a frustrating situation for a single male who is visiting from abroad and who is too shy to attempt intimacy. To add to that, one can see the 'great Indian back rub' on display all the time. This doesn't require special chairs or beds. It is practised by big-breasted young Indian women who lean forward onto the backs of their male motorbike riders, even when the bike isn't in motion. And when the bike is in motion, you can imagine the whirring action of those breasts etching concentric and parabolic rings of ecstasy onto the backs of these blessed males.

So, after a week or ten days of ravenous epidermal hunger and total lack of contact with the opposite sex, I was desperate to be touched. And yet, oh the folly of having gone to a massage place whose number I had obtained from the *Times of India* classifieds.

There was one thing the masseuse, whose name was Uma and who said she came from Shimoga and had worked there for two months, did reasonably well. This was the way she massaged my crack and my balls—softly, tenderly, with the respect due to Their Highnesses, unlike the Ayurvedic male human pistons; if only the gooey cream she used didn't make me feel messy, as if I had dirtied or wet myself, it would have been perfect. I was aroused and hot as hell, yet not willing to let her triumph by jacking me off. She tried to, and seemed smug that she could get me to spurt in seconds . . . and failed. Because there was something so crude about her manner and demeanour, it was as if she betrayed a consciousness of original sin, and of shame about what she was doing. Poor thing, it was her loss, but she had in her not a fraction of that joy of sex and playfulness with the opposite sex that you find in Thai and Indonesian women.

Playfulness and joy? Forget it. Even a serious, somber massage from a woman to a man in a big Indian city costs nothing less than a thousand rupees an hour. However, one may be luckier, pricewise (and possibly otherwise), in a smaller town. In 2003, I had made contact in Mangalore with Sonia, saried, long hair tied in a severe bun, no make-up, a nurse aged around fifty, who worked in the physiotherapy department of a hospital. She came over to my 3.5-star Swapna Mahal hotel room—with relative ease, for she was at the age when the hotel staff wouldn't stop her or 'suspect' her, as they might a woman in her twenties (the prejudice in these parts being that after forty or forty-five, women cease to be sexual beings). Fleshy but not fat, she was good enough—slow, smooth, relaxed, even coolly sensuous. Because she didn't have to go anywhere, it being a holiday, and only 11 a.m. in the morning, so feeling generous, she spontaneously tried to massage my penis, to which I quickly told her: *No, I don't like that, and though I do like sex, I have a girlfriend.* I said this to connect with her at a human level, so to speak, rather than keep an aloof and superior demeanour. I told her my girlfriend would like to marry me, at which Eunice responded firmly: 'Don't tell her that. Don't marry her. Tell her you would just like to keep it to friendship.' I paid her three hundred rupees, for she kneaded me for a full hour, and I felt it was deserved.

But a few months later in Bangalore, in the cantonment area of the city, I discovered a more enlightened massage place. Here, in a house located in a compound with trees, the rates varied depending on whether or not you needed your little brother milked (or watered?)—in other words, if you wanted a McLingam Junior (the rough, poor man's version of a lingam massage). It was this place I used constantly for the next two years, with happy results (and rare 'happy endings'), but I did have occasional moments of irritation, as the one that follows.

The female masseuses of Bangalore all have their principles, and you better not try to fuck them. Those who suck will not fuck, and those who lick nipples will not suck dick, and those who fuck will never take you from behind (okay, I am getting carried away by my satirical mood here—that last phrase is pure fiction), and those who will only 'make your water come out' won't give you much of a massage anyway. So I was asked if I needed my 'heat released'. The girl, Vanita, a Christian from Mangalore, then conspiratorially informed me that the other establishments allowed all kinds of depraved nonsense, but not they—they were sisters of charity, no less admirable and philanthropic than the members of Mother Teresa's order, who confined themselves to the noble enterprise of reducing male global warming by cooling their male customers' 'heat'.

At this same massage place during a later visit, I was massaged by Rosita, a Manipuri. She rested her left hand on my buttocks, so casually, as if it were a cushion meant as a hand rest. As if it were a handle to hold on to for balance while she used her other arm to massage my lower back.

And then one day, a year later—boy, India was zooming into modernity and looseness, thanks to the anonymity and widespread penetration of mobile phones. I dipped into one of the local 'Free Ads' weeklies and found an ad for a Bangalore massage service which offered 'home delivery'—perhaps inspired by the entry into India of Domino's Pizza. The girl, possibly around twenty-one and saried, Tamilian, smiling and sweet-natured, arrived with a thirty-fivish, aunty-ish female handler or companion who waited in the anteroom while her associate massaged my posterior in the poste-room. From her, I received a competent and sincere massage, the girl assuring me that 'we don't worry about five minutes extra, we finish the job'. However as she finished, she asked, demurely and solemnly, 'Does anything have to be done for the private parts?'

'Madam,' I replied, rather formally. 'I am a writer. I have no private parts.'

Now for a recent advertisement I quote in entirety from a personal column, misspellings included, having changed only the name and leaving out the phone number:

> Hi, this Lokesh from chennai my age his 33. I am doing massage for past 8 year . i should not say about my work u try with me once u do massage with me u will be calling me again: .LINGAM MASSAGE, YONI MASSAGE, BREAST MASSAGE AND BODY RELAXATION MASSAGE WITH AYURVEDA OIL FOR LADIES AND GENTLEMEN AND COUPLES AT CHENNAI DOORSTEP SERVICE.
>
> My 'style' is Swedish, Esalen, Zen shiatsu, hot jade stone therapy. Similar to 'Lomi Lomi' and Esalen massage relaxing and deepening by a fluid connection. I work from my heart.

Come to experience a Professional Therapeutic Massage that will relieve stress, tension, and aching muscles and brighten your spirit. My massage is very intuitive to disperse blocked energy, a blend of aromatherapy, soft effleurage, acupressure, Thai stretching, deep tissue, and integrate all your mind, and spirit. Every massage session meet your needs.

They all love spending time with true gentlemen and are eager to please.

Call me at phone xxx-xxxxxxx.

Rate its chep not to high rate

Try once.

Amen. Breast and yoni massage from a true gentleman, and at 'chep' rates to boot. You've come a long way, ye oppressed babies of India.

INTERLUDE 3

IN PRAISE OF PRETENDED ANATOMICAL IGNORANCE

You would think that an ignorance of anatomy would be a crushing disqualification for a masseuse. In general, your hunch would be correct. But in reality, a partial innocence about the male anatomy (mostly pretended, I realized later—never underestimate the intelligence of women, and don't ever forget that their superior peripheral vision and intuition can leave us men in the dust) can result in lots of good, clean fun, meaningful laughs as well as pleasure for all parties concerned, including for the male being massaged by a woman. It always delights me to notice how often a right-leaning or left-leaning penis manages to sneak up on an anatomically innocent masseuse and take her by surprise, and how despite all her attempts at assuring modesty and propriety, the cunning penis lies in wait and ambushes the lovely hand which, until that moment, had been determined to touch only your boringly legal parts.

The secret is this (and please *do* make a donation towards my research fund if you are a masseuse and obtained this secret from me): As in politics, so in essential anatomy, very few men are true centrists. Nearly all of us have penises that lean mainly either to the right or the left. My own dick doesn't even know its own mind: most often, like my political views, it leans to the left; but at other times, inexplicably, it will decide—also like my political views—to lean towards the right. At still other times it leans towards the far-right or far-left, rarely even going for a reactionary south-western inclination, surprising even me, its owner, while on still other occasions, it gets into a playful mood and tries to imitate a low-flying but stationary cruise missile, its shaft hovering just about one inch above my thigh. Why this is so is a mystery I cannot explain, though a probable theory is that it, having a will and an agenda of its own, is trying to hypnotize the masseuse into taking off her clothes and getting into bed with me. You wouldn't expect it of such a tiny fellow, one who doesn't seem to come equipped with any brains, but it/he is a wily seducer, one who outshines me by far.

I have in recent years connected with a woman who has been massaging me naked. Meaning, *I* am fully naked; having started formally with a towel guarding the crown jewels, at some point we decided there were no secrets left, that everything I had to show had been seen umpteen times, and to cover myself was sheer laughable hypocrisy and a waste of towels, which, as I was single, I would have to launder myself.

Now this woman, who I shall call Smitha, has even pointed out to me, after long observation and careful study over the course of perhaps fifty massages with her, that my penis follows her in whichever direction she goes while massaging me. And she really is proud of it, it being amusing and flattering to her at the same time—a feather in her cap, if she had a cap (and which, she being a south Indian lady in a sari, would have looked ridiculous with). And I must admit she is right most of the time, though the wily little thing foils all predictions, including hers.

In any case, as we are comfortable with each other, most of the time this is a game that helps us pass the time and squeeze a few laughs out of the unfathomable absurd, which Camus used up many books and trees, and much valuable time, trying to explain. But with the combination of a new and innocent masseuse and a towel or bed sheet, the results can be surprisingly delightful. Because a woman who massages you naked but mechanically is far less erotically arousing than a woman who massages you while you are well-covered, but accidentally touches your penis (and secretly, you have been yearning for that touch—it may have been nearly half the point of the massage).

Most Western masseuses will expertly slide the edge of the towel over your penis and around it and then wedge the edge of the towel under your other thigh, thus quarantining your penis and reducing any risk of accidental contact by 98 per cent. But this rarely happens with Southeast Asian masseuses, who are more prone to happy accidents (and also, perhaps not so incidentally, to 'happy endings'). Possibly, they enjoy these accidents as much as the men do—and it is all a grown-up version of the game of hide-and-seek that can endlessly delight a child, and eternal children like me.

EPILOGUE: HOW A MASSEUSE MAY SAVE YOUR LIFE, AND WHY MASSAGE IS BOOMING

In a Filipino town not far from Manila, in a massage shop tucked away amidst the clatter of jeepneys, traffic and loud music coming out of assorted shops, it was twenty-sixish Rea, who has the broad benevolent face of a Buddha, and is always generous and unstinting with her shy but broad and heartfelt smiles, like sunshine breaking through the clouds, who finally brought home to me how a truly good masseuse may end up saving your life.

I have for some years now been having around one hundred and fifty massages a year, which is possible and affordable in certain countries of Asia—even in India, if you are able to directly connect and make a regular arrangement with a simple masseuse, bypassing bloodsucking intermediaries who cheat Indian masseuses of most of their income.

And yet it was Rea who became the first masseuse in some months to touch my groin, to touch it feelingly, and to discover a bump there—what could be a cyst or a tumor. It was something the others hadn't noticed, even though they may have touched me there. It was something even my lovers hadn't noticed (bad, bad girls!).

And why did Rea find this bump while the others didn't? Because she has such a pure mind, the issues of sex or modesty simply didn't enter her head. The others lack the Zen quality of being in the moment, of being at every moment fully and 100 per cent occupied with the thing that they are doing, and nothing else. Even while massaging you, they may be chatting with the masseuse in the next cubicle perhaps, or listening to music, or perhaps to the music in their head, remembering some argument they had with a boyfriend, or complimenting themselves on their rote-like technique, while forgetting to concentrate on the person on the table and the specific contours and vibrations emanating from the part they are working on.

Whereas, when Rea is feeling your body, she is also *feeling for* your body. Her compassion is nurturing, like a concerned and loving mother's, and she was able to zero in on a problem that even I had missed, because even I don't go thoroughly over all the parts of my body, palpating each separate square inch to see where something might be amiss. When I am in the shower, I am hurriedly soaping myself and trying to get done with this unavoidable, but not necessarily ecstatic, task as quickly as possible, and just making broad moves with my hands to get the soap on and then off, trying to handle large swathes of flesh in one stroke.

As for doctors these days, they are afraid even to shake your hand. Even with their sensation-deadening gloves on, their hands race over your body, only examining the spots that *you* point out to them. This is quite unlike Rea, who owns your body while she is massaging it; once you have implicitly given her your permission by showing her your trust, she checks it thoroughly.

Not spouses. Spouses may simply go for the main parts: the attractive parts of your body, your Venices and Taj Mahals and Eiffel Towers, while leaving out the Rwandas and Chads and Three Mile Canals, areas that are hidden or not easily within reach in the normal face-to-face coupling positions (which itself may be a good reason to engage in the sixty-nine and other bizarrely angled *Kamasutra* positions, including the standing on one's head, every now and then, notwithstanding the inconvenience or the risk of bursting into laughter and losing your erection).

And so, your masseuse may one day save your life. In addition to delivering not negligible daily benefits such as boosting your immunity, giving you stress relief (yes, stress kills), and making you feel more human. But only if the masseuse is good, caring, and is in it for more than just the money. That is why I think this is an important book, passionately making the case not just for having technically proficient and caring massages, but for good, unobstructed and broadminded massages, and also for the exchange of massages between couples—a one-week course in 'How to Massage Your Lover' ought to be a prerequisite for granting a marriage licence. Well, if not a prerequisite, then at least entitling one to a cash benefit.

Should there be any doubt in your mind regarding its therapeutic benefits, the highly reputed Mayo Clinic in Minnesota has this assurance on its website: 'Brush aside any thoughts that massage is only a feel-good way to indulge or pamper yourself. To the contrary, massage can be a powerful tool to help you take charge of your health and well-being, whether you have a specific health condition or are just looking for another stress reliever.'

As I write this epilogue, I realize that the law of diminishing returns applies to massages as well as to love affairs and ice creams—when you have had 3,500 of anything, you probably won't be as ecstatic about the 3501st one as you were for the first and the hundredth. But my enthusiasm in principle for excellent, humanistic massages, and their importance to mankind, has not diminished.

To sum up: I am all for clarity, honesty and a lack of hypocrisy, and for the right of both the masseuse and the customer to choose the massage he or she wants to be a part of, without coercion or big brotherly restrictions, provided the giver of a non-sexual massage is technically proficient and does not make the customer feel like a criminal. One way to reduce the possibility of embarrassment for women therapists is to have properly advertised and legalized sensual massage widely available everywhere, so that men will not go where they are unwelcome (just as smokers do not willingly choose hotels where smoking is prohibited). It would also help if the former group clearly advertised their services as non-sexual and, if they so preferred, to confine their practices to other women.

But following years of experience, reflection and initial denial on my own part, I now believe that but for the abundance of sexual starvation, and but for men not getting enough sex, and perhaps almost equally often, women not getting enough sex (and the sex of their fantasies besides), the demand for massages would plummet to perhaps one-fourth their present number—and the demand crash would result in far cheaper regular massages. After all, many licenced massage therapists, even those studying the subject for a year and a half (and many have done much shorter courses), have less than half the education of an average registered nurse, who starts at about $18 an hour in the US. In India, the average massage from a woman costs one thousand rupees per hour, and most nurses barely earn a few hundred rupees in an entire day. It is the sexual and intimate quality of massage, and its feeding of the human hunger for nurturing touch, that gives it a premium far beyond its labour value. (I do not, of course, speak of outstanding masseuses, who deserve to be valued and rewarded like goddesses.)

However, such an ideal society is still far from realization, and sexual starvation, at least to a mild degree, is probably going to continue for a long, long time in most of the world, and to a much greater degree in India. Meanwhile, as the inhibitions and hypocrisy surrounding massage gradually diminish, my guess is that massage establishments will continue to boom and prices will not fall significantly anytime soon.

You could say I am a dreamer (and yes, that John Lennon song and the Beatles in general have influenced my thinking in a major way). But allow me, please, to give voice to my dream: that we return to a more intimate form of society, one in which massages are exchanged, bartered or donated free in volunteer service, in temples of skin-love, in much the same way that once upon a time, in ancient Rome and even in India, temple courtesans freely gave their bodies to devotees in honour of the god or goddess they served. (For in the end, as the final Beatles song goes, '*the love you take is equal to the love you make*'.)

Note that it is not only men who derive sexual pleasure from massages. I once met a lesbian who massages only women—because she's getting paid for her pleasure, besides doubling her chance for a Saturday night date.

Meanwhile, until the problem of global sexual famine, which afflicts billions (though some of them might be unaware of it, or unwilling to admit it), and which underlies much war, aggression, hatred, cheating and genocide, is solved, it is cruel and even dangerous for authorities to stop, curtail or harass the relatively mild and benevolent relative of sex that is massage in its various forms.

On the other hand, in countries without legal hurdles to massage, there has been an increasing tendency to over-commercialize, the worst examples of which I consider to be expensive and yuppie-serving spas and the great American body rub franchises, where the menu includes items such as just neck and shoulders, or just back, as if the rest of the body were some pariah, and other brain-fractured outfits that sell parts-specific massage—just neck, just back, just feet, just thighs. All of which seems to corrupt the original spirit of massage (when will they start offering massage just for the middle finger or the right ear lobe I wonder). To capitalistically exploit massage (as takeover specialists buy up mammoth corporations, chop them up into tiny parts, and sell these parts for huge profits) is no better than to sell sex or to sell water or to sell love—things which, in an ideal world, should never be sold.

Meanwhile, masseuses deserve to make a decent living, like school teachers, like caregivers to the weak (children and old people), like single mothers and single fathers. And the givers of superb, compassionate massages deserve to be respected as goddesses, and are far more deserving of a comfortable standard of living than CEOs who rip up companies and run Ponzi schemes. But the over-commercialization of massage has attracted many of the wrong type into the profession, including some who actually have no empathy for their fellow human beings, but who see it more as a quick money-milking (or customer-milking) business than as a vocation or a mission.

It has also attracted the wrong type of entrepreneurs: sharks. In 1999, in a beautiful resort north of San Francisco, a masseuse confessed to me that her share of the $80 massage fee was just $25. This is unconscionable—it should be illegal for any establishment to pocket more than 30 per cent of a massage therapist's fee, no matter what its excuse. I am sure the same is true in India.

Meanwhile, as the West and the metropolitan centres in the East become more prosperous and more liberal in theory, more and more people there and in the dizzily developing and rat-racing sections of the developing world, infected by the globalization bug, lead lives of lonely, neurotic and touch-less desperation (as powerfully depicted in *Atomised* by French writer Michel Houellebecq). Therefore, massage ought to be encouraged and subsidized as a humanistic, philanthropic activity, and as a legitimate branch of medical and psychiatric treatment.

The Beatles, and John Lennon, got it almost right. '*All you need is love*' might be a bit of an oversimplification as a philosophy of life, but it is a worthwhile ideal, one that we need to counter the increasing prevalence of the commercial instinct, according to which nothing, not even a bottle of water or a luggage cart (as at Heathrow airport), can be had for free, an instinct epitomized in the famous saying: No money, no honey.

Finally, a personal note: I began with a personal story, telling you something about the 'I' that gets all these massages, but then restricted the narrative to the massages themselves. Some of you might think this unfair, while others might think it appropriate—this was, after all, supposed to be a tour of the massage world in which I merely happened to be a reporter, guide, guinea pig, occasional philosopher and chronicler of experience.

However, to provide the first group with a brief update or conclusion to an unfinished and continuing story: I remember many women in my life, and I've loved them all—some a little less, and some a little more; some have massaged me, some have not. And one of them still comes to me in my dreams, and is almost the only one to do so. I don't always understand it—maybe, in some mysterious way, she symbolizes the eternal woman or feminine principle that I love through all the other women I have loved since.

It is not a neat ending, but unlike romantic movies and commercial novels, life rarely has neat endings—and this is my life.

ACKNOWLEDGEMENTS

I wish to acknowledge the following persons who helped me with their support, by reading the book and by encouraging me to persevere, to complete it, and to share it with the world: Karthika V.K., Publisher and Chief Editor, HarperCollins India, and Alexander Von Prellwitz of Eulama Literary Agency, who was my agent for a full year and who gave me exceptional encouragement and support for this book during that time. Also, Debasri Rakshit of HarperCollins India, who did a fine and brave job of editing a complex manuscript and supporting the writer at the same time; and many other good friends of mine who have stood by me through the ups and downs in my literary career, and who are too numerous to name. And above all, a big thank you to you, my readers, who believe in books and in independent writers, and without whom no writer can hope to survive and carry on with his or her dream.